Anne Rice's Unauthorized French Quarter Tour

*Featuring the Vampire and
Mayfair Witches Chronicles*

BY THAT OTHER TOUR LLC

First Printing, 2012
Printed in the United States of America

Paperback
ISBN: 1-938734-03-3
ISBN: 978-1-938734-03-8

Kindle Version
ISBN-10: 1-938734-00-9
ISBN-13: 978-1-938734-00-7

Nook Version
ISBN-10: 1-938734-01-7
ISBN-13: 978-1-938734-01-4

iPad, iPhone and iTouch Version
ISBN-10: 1-938734-02-5
ISBN-13: 978-1-938734-02-1

Sony Reader Version
ISBN: 1-938734-05-X
ISBN: 978-1-938734-05-2

Smashwords Version
ISBN-10: 1-938734-04-1
ISBN-13: 978-1-938734-04-5

Acknowledgments

This book would not have been possible without the support of many people. That Other Tour LLC wishes to express their gratitude to Anne Rice for writing great novels with so many great historical locations in New Orleans. Deepest gratitude is also due to the Historic New Orleans Collection and the Williams Research Center for use of their great resources and assistance for which this tour book would not have been successful. Special thanks also to Nancy Lockyear who took me to my first Anne Rice Vampire Lestat Fan Club Ball at the State Palace Theatre in 1999. Thanks Diane and Karen for doing whatever whim I had such as going plantation hopping and going out with me on a whim. The author would also like to convey thanks to Saralyn, Priestess Miriam Chamani, Virginia Ann B. Dengel and everyone at the Rink. The author wishes to express her love and gratitude to her beloved family for their support.

For more information about Anne Rice's Unauthorized Tours, please visit the following:

	http://www.annericetours.com
	http://www.facebook.com/AnneRiceTours
	http://twitter.com/AnneRiceTours
	http://youtube.com/AnneRiceTour
	http://myspace.com/AnneRiceTours

We are not associated with Anne Rice the writer.

Dedicated

To My Best Friend

G M Higgs

Contents

Beginning of Tour 20

Jackson Square 21

Pontalba Buildings 24

Lower Pontalba Apartments 25

The Presbytere 26

Pere Antoine Alley 29

St. Louis Cathedral 31

Pirate's Alley 33

The Cabildo 35

Upper Pontalba Apartments 37

Jackson Brewery 38

Dixie Gates 41

Washington Artillery Park 43

Café du Monde 45

Central Grocery Company.................................... 48

Gallatin Street 51

French Market... 53

Govenor Nicholls & Esplanade Wharfs.................... 55

Esplanade Avenue.. 57

Faubourg Marigny.. 59

Bayou Road 61

Gallier House 63

Old Ursuline Convent... 65

Condé Street Ballroom 67

Dumaine Street 68

Librairie Book Shop 69

Voodoo Occult Shops 71

Madame John's Legacy... 72

700 - 900 Rue Royal... 74

St Ann Street 75

Theatre d'Orleans... 76

Crescent City Cigar Shop 79

Bourbon Street... 81

Court of Two Sisters.. 83

French Opera House 85

Hermann-Grima House 87

Antoine's Restaurant 89

WDSU-TV Front Entrance..................................... 91

St Louis Hotel... 92

Third Precinct Police Station 94

Quarter Smith 96

Pharmacy Museum 98

WDSU TV Rear Entrance..................................... 100

Moonwalk..102

Steamboat Natchez.......................................104

Woldenberg Park...106

Audubon Aquarium of the Americas.............108

Canal Street - Algiers Ferry..........................110

New Orleans Passport Agency........................113

Tipitina's...114

Boyer Antiques & Doll Shop..........................116

Hotel Monteleone..118

Hurwitz Mintz Furniture..............................120

Solan's Grocery...122

Pickwick Club...124

French, Spanish and American Streets............127

Kolb's Restaurant..129

Marks Isaacs...130

F. W. Woolworth Co......................................132

Katz and Besthoff (K&B) Drugstore.............135

St. Charles Streetcar Stop..............................137

Gus Mayer..139

Galatoire's Restaurant...................................141

Desire Oyster Bar..144

D. H. Holmes..146

Godchaux's 148

Maison Blanche 150

S.H. Kress & Company 153

The Ritz-Carlton 154

Loew's State Palace Theatre 155

Union Station 156

Storyville 158

St. Louis Cemetery 1 160

Our Lady of Guadalupe Church 163

Charity Hospital 165

The Ramparts - Back of Town - Tremé 166

Municipal Auditorium 168

Conclusion 170

Recommendation 171

Introduction

Anne Rice's Unauthorized French Quarter Tour is a historical fiction tour that blends old New Orleans with present-day New Orleans. This tour only covers the Vampire Chronicles and Mayfair Witches novels.

Anne Rice's notoriety as a writer began when Interview with the Vampire, the first book in the Vampire Chronicles, made its debut in 1976. Anne published several books prior to Interview with the Vampire, but none grabbed the imagination of the reader in the same way. The book went on to become a major motion picture starring Tom Cruise and Brad Pitt. Anne also wrote three books about another supernatural family, the Mayfair Witches.

The French Quarter (Vieux Carré), New Orleans' (La Nouvelle-Orléans) first city, was established in 1718 by French Canadian naval officer Jean Baptiste Bienville. The French Quarter plays a significant role in Anne Rice's novels. It's the place where her characters live, dine, shop, and enjoy the opera and other entertainment.

Interestingly enough, the Vampire Chronicles and the Mayfair Witches had many parallels until they crossed paths in Blackwood Farm. For example, Lestat and Marie Claudette Mayfair arrived in La Nouvelle-Orléans in the same year, 1789. Their lives began in New Orleans after family members were killed during the French Revolution. Both spoke French before speaking English. Lestat settled in the savage garden known as the Vieux Carré, a place we now know as the French Quarter. Marie Claudette built her primary home, La Victoire plantation, at the Riverbend, but also had a home in the French Quarter, not too far from Lestat, Louis, and Claudia. The area Marie Claudette fled parallels the history of Haiti in 1789, and La Victoire is a real place in Haiti.

Characters in both books attended the same Quadroon Balls, enjoyed the same theatres, frequented the same riverfront bars, lived in the same hotels, and owned homes in the same area in the French Quarter and Garden District. Anne not only chronicled the lives of the central characters, but also the actual names of the streets, shops, neighborhoods, and types of transportation in favor at that period in time.

The French Quarter (Vieux Carré) is bounded by the Mississippi River, North Rampart and Canal Streets, and Esplanade Avenue. This tour will cover the French Quarter, the original city, a portion of the American District (Canal Street only) and a small portion of "The Ramparts", which is known today as Tremé.

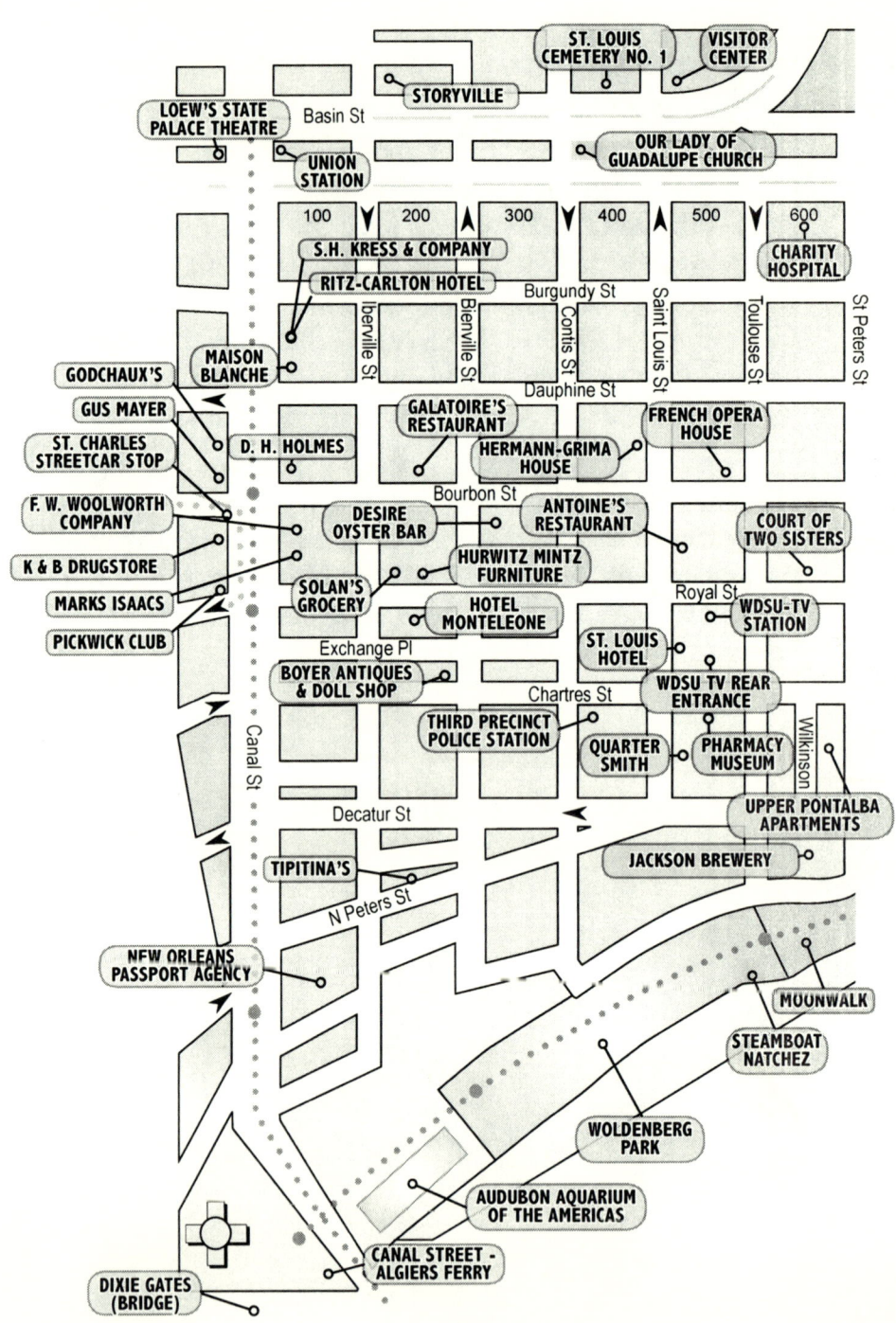

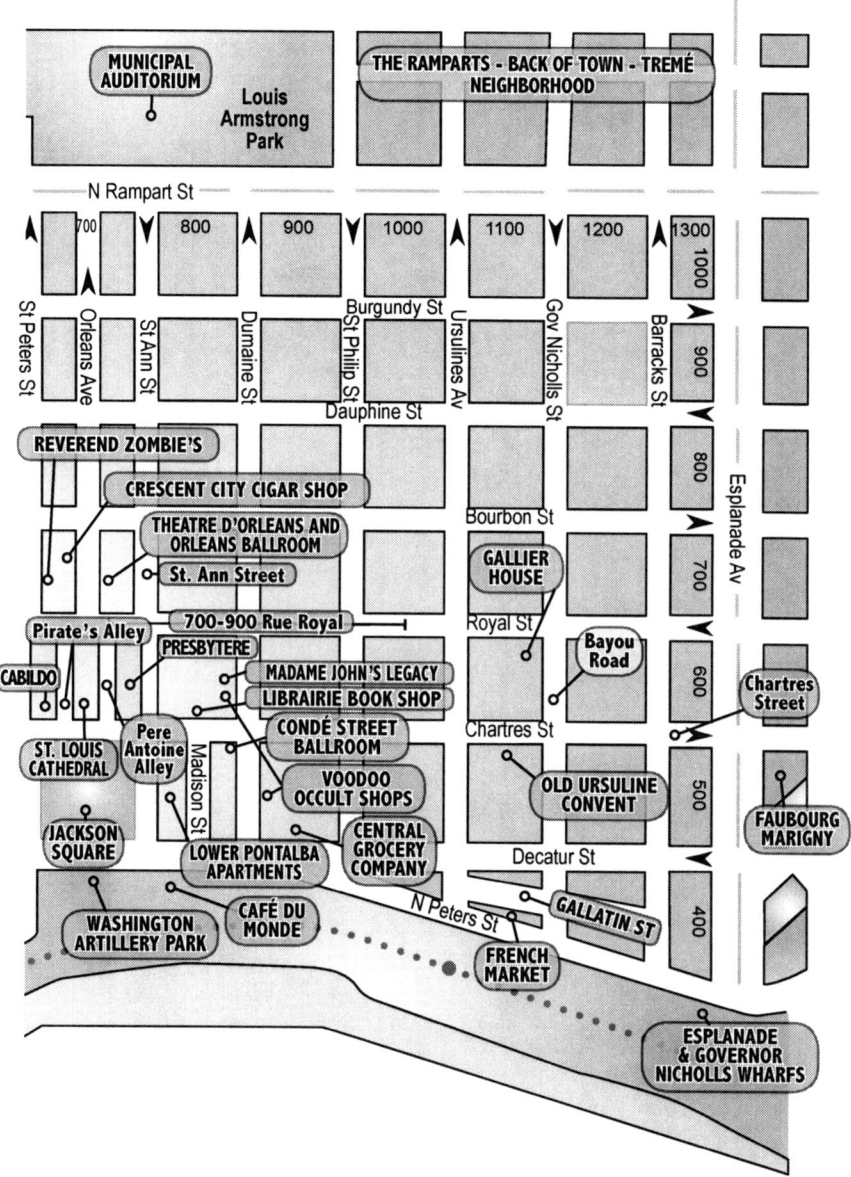

Notes

Legend

Throughout this book you will see two-letter abbreviations at the end of some descriptions. These abbreviations refer to the name of the book(s) associated with the event, which are as follows:

- Vampire Chronicles - VC
- Interview with the Vampire - IV
- Vampire Lestat - VL
- Queen of the Damned - QD
- Tale of the Body Thief - BT
- Memnoch the Devil - MD
- Vampire Armand - VA
- Merrick - MR
- Blood and Gold - BG
- Blackwood Farm - BF
- Blood Canticle - BC
- Mayfair Trilogy
- Witching Hour - WH
- Lasher - LR
- Taltos - TS
- Movie
- Anne Rice Biography – Bio

Beginning of Tour

The tour will start in Jackson Square next to the equestrian statue of Andrew Jackson. Jackson Square is between the Mississippi River (Decatur Street) and the front entrance of the St Louis Cathedral (Chartres Street), and between the Upper Pontalba (St. Peter Street) and Lower (St. Ann Street) Pontalba Apartments. If you have problems finding Jackson Square, ask any doorman or store clerk. Make your way to Jackson Square.

Directions 1

If you can't go inside Jackson Square, go to the gate in front of St. Louis Cathedral.

Jackson Square

Jackson Square is a historic park, originally known as the Place d'Armes. The centerpiece of Jackson Square is a statue of its namesake, General Andrew Jackson, sitting in noble grandeur upon his horse. In January 1851, the city council changed the name from Place d'Armes to Jackson Square in honor of the hero of the Battle of New Orleans. Modeled after the picturesque Place des Vosges in Paris, the square is a tribute to the city's rich historical heritage. If you look at the buildings that surround Jackson Square, you will see many of New Orleans' architectural gems. Not only are the buildings beautiful, but many, like the lovely Cabildo (old city hall) served as a backdrop for significant events in the history of the city, state, and country.

The focal point of Jackson Square is the stunning St. Louis Cathedral. The triple steeples that rise above the park have become the hallmark of the oldest Catholic Cathedral in continuous use in the United States. Flanked by its neighbors, the Cabildo on the left and the Presbytere on the right, the cathedral is a popular destination for tourists, particularly the religious, and a well-loved spot for weddings.

> Dr. Petrie saw Lasher in broad daylight, standing motionless on the grass in Jackson Square. WH

> Jackson Square is the first place Lestat sees body thief Raglan James and directs James to meet him in old French Market at the other side of the square. BT

> The scene where Claudia is sitting on a bench waiting for a victim, and other scenes in the film Interview with the Vampire, were filmed in Jackson Square. Movie

> Fledging vampire Mona Mayfair broke away from Lestat and Quinn and went wandering along Jackson Square, having a great time in Aunt Queen's high-heeled shoes. BC

> Jesse Reeves, who was investigating the Royal Street townhouse for the Talamasca, took time to enjoy Jackson Square. QD

> On the night Lestat and Louis took Claudia from the hospital, Lestat stopped briefly under a lamp, where Louis caught up with him, near Jackson Square. IV

- Lestat, famous author and rock star, was often offered blood from fans that spotted him in Jackson Square. BT

- Michael Curry and Marie Louise celebrated Mardi Gras, dressed as pirates, in Jackson Square making out. WH

- When Lestat returned to New Orleans from Armand's villa on Night Island, his first stop was Jackson Square. QD

Directions 2

Take a look at the two apartment buildings to the right and left of Jackson Square. These are the Pontalba Buildings.

Pontalba Buildings

The two matching four-story redbrick apartment buildings bordering Jackson Square are known as the Upper and Lower Pontalba Apartments. These apartments were renovated in the 1830s and 1840s, when Jackson Square was known as Place D'Armes. Many consider these two buildings to be the oldest apartment units in the United States. However, before they were fifty apartment units, they were sixteen row houses (adjacent uniform units), and later townhouses (adjacent non-uniform units). Baroness Micaela Almonaster Pontalba inherited the land bordering Jackson Square and all buildings on the land from her father, Andres Almonaster y Rojas, who speculated in real estate. Unhappy with the condition of the square, the Baroness renovated the buildings into the most expensive apartments in New Orleans, supervising everything. James Gallier was the first architect hired to design the townhouses. He was replaced with Henry Howard. The Baroness would often climb up and down scaffolding to check the builders' work. If you look closely you will see "AP" entwined in the cast iron railings of the galleries. This stands for Almonaster and Pontalba.

The Pontalba Apartments were declared a National Historic Landmark on May 30, 1974.

Directions 3

Turn and face St. Louis Cathedral and walk until you are outside Jackson Square gates. Look right, towards the apartment building on the corner of Chartres and St. Ann Streets.

Lower Pontalba Apartments

Clem picked up Quinn Blackwood and Mona Mayfair at the corner of Chartres and St. Ann Streets by the Lower Pontalba to take them back to Blackwood Farm. BC

Directions 4

Look at the large building caddy corner to the apartments (across from Jackson Square).

The Presbytere

The Presbytere is one of twin Spanish colonial-style buildings that stand on the right side (lower/down-river side) of the St. Louis Cathedral, along Jackson Square, at the corner of St. Ann and Chartres Streets. The Presbytere was designed to match the Cabildo on the other side of the St. Louis Cathedral. The Presbytere was built around 1790 as a home for the Capuchin monks who were living in a building fronting Cloister's Alley (now called Pere Antoine Alley) prior to the fire of 1788. In 1790, Don Andres Almonaster y Rojas began construction on a replacement building and called it the Casa Curial. In French, Presbytere translates into "residence for the clergy serving the parish church."

In 1794, a fire destroyed the second building, and Almonaster once again paid to have the building replaced. Almonaster died in 1798, leaving only the first floor done. The building's construction was eventually completed in 1813. It was never used as a rectory, but was rented and then purchased in 1853 by the city to be used as a courthouse under the Spanish, and later, under the Americans. Today, the Presbytere is part of the Louisiana State Museum. The Presbytere became part of the National Register of Historic Places on April 15, 1970.

> Talamasca members Aaron Lightner and Mary took a young Merrick Mayfair to various museums. The Presbytere is most likely one of the museums Merrick visited. MR

Directions 5

Take a look at the wide alley between the Presbytere and St. Louis Cathedral. This is Pere Antoine Alley.

Pere Antoine Alley

In the beginning, Pere Antoine Alley was known as Cloister Alley because of the small Capuchin Monastery built here during the early years of the Louisiana Colony. The original Capuchin Monastery and buildings were destroyed by the fire of 1788. Other names associated with the alley were St. Anthony Street, the Passage de Saint Antoine, and Saint Anthony's Alley. In 1831, city plans changed, and Orleans Street stopped at Royal Street. Two passageways or alleys were cut to create a passage from Jackson Square to Royal Street. The alleys were named Ruelle d'Orleans Nord (North) and Ruelle d'Orleans Sud (South). Neither name seemed to stick. People continued to call it Cloister Alley or St. Anthony's Alley. On February, 20, 1924, the alley's name was officially changed to Pere Antoine Alley in honor of Padre Antonio de Sedella, later known as Pere Antoine, a beloved Capuchin monk and former pastor of St. Louis Cathedral, at that time called St. Louis Church.

> Pere Antoine Alley appears in the movie Interview with the Vampire. Movie

Directions 6

To the left of the Pere Antoine Alley is perhaps one of the most recognizable landmarks in New Orleans, the St. Louis Cathedral.

St. Louis Cathedral

Perhaps one of the most recognizable landmarks in New Orleans, the St. Louis Cathedral, stands in all its glory, welcoming visitors to the Crescent City. It was originally called St. Louis Church. Today it's known as the Basilica of St. Louis, King of France. The cathedral is the oldest continuously operating cathedral in the United States. Located on the Chartres Street side of Jackson Square, the three steeples of St. Louis Cathedral rise dramatically into the New Orleans sky. Facing Decatur Street and the mighty Mississippi River, the church stands as a beacon of light over the historic French Quarter. The streets around the cathedral are named after saints.

Not only is the cathedral the seat of the Roman Catholic Archdiocese of New Orleans, it has also been visited by Popes, presidents, and dignitaries. Its position on a public square indicates the importance that the Catholic religion played in the early days of New Orleans. A Roman Catholic Church has stood on this spot since 1718. The first one was an early colonial structure made of wood. In 1726, a larger brick edifice was constructed, only to be destroyed in the Great New Orleans Fire in 1788. A series of other structures was built on the site, with the current church completed in 1850. The bell from an earlier tower, built in 1819, still remains in use.

For one block, from St. Ann to St. Peter Streets, Chartres Street's name changed to Place John Paul II in honor of Pope John Paul II's visit to New Orleans in 1987.

▸ Louis brother was buried from the old church on this spot before he was taken to the cemetery. IV

▸ Louis confesses his sins, murder of thousands, to the priest at St. Louis Cathedral, just before he kills him on the steps to the Communion rail. IV

▸ Lestat said the St. Louis Church at the Place d'Armes was tiny compared to the one we see today. IV

▸ The downtown and French Mayfair's worshiped and marry at the St Louis Cathedral. WH

▸ Beatrice Mayfair and Aaron Lightner have a quiet wedding at St. Louis Cathedral. LS

▸ Lionel Mayfair, and uptown relative, began to appear at mass at the St Louis Cathedral with one of the downtown cousins. LS

▸ Louis met Lestat the night before he made the body switch in Jackson Square. BT

▸ Lestat breaks into St. Louis Cathedral twice, once before he makes the body switch with and when he recovers his body from Raglan James. Each time he meets Louis and it s here Lestat asks Louis to come live with him once again. BT

▸ Lynelle, Quinn's tutor, takes Quinn to the St. Louis Cathedral to light a candle and say a prayer. BF

Directions 7

The alley to the left of the St. Louis Cathedral is Pirate's Alley.

Pirate's Alley

The infamous Pirate's Alley is a place of legend and lore. It was once called Orleans Alley South, an extension of Orleans Street. How it got the name Pirate's Alley is a bit of a mystery.

You will rarely find it on any street maps. Although it's a well-known fact the name was officially changed from Orleans Alley to Pirate's Alley in 1964, some city directories continue to list the alley by its original name.

How it got the name Pirate's Alley is a bit of a mystery. Most likely "Pirate" was the name of a prominent person or family living in the alley. Or, Pirate was a well-known establishment located in the alley. Or, the Pirate's office, (a company or person(s) who reproduced documents by hand (such as deeds, contracts or other court/legal documents) before the copy machine was invented) was located in the alley. We do know that this unassuming alley dates back to 1831. Its most famous resident was novelist William Faulkner, who lived at 624 Orleans Alley, and wrote his first book, Soldiers' Pay, there in the 1920s.

> Claudia revealed her plans to kill Lestat to Louis when they were walking in Pirate's Alley. IV

Directions 8

To the left of Pirates Alley is the Cabildo.

The Cabildo

The Cabildo was once used by the local government. It's now part of the Louisiana State Museum. The land on which the Cabildo sits was once a Town Hall, several libraries, a fire station, the place where the French flag was lowered and the American flag raised, a jail and police station, and police court, along with several government offices—including but not limited to City Hall and the Supreme Court of the State of Louisiana. This is the building where, in 1803, the transfer of Louisiana from Spain to France took place and twenty days later, its transfer from France to the United States. You can walk in the rooms where the Louisiana Purchase was signed in 1803, and see the main hall that was once used as a courtroom.

The Cabildo has withstood the test of time, including being destroyed in 1788 by the Great New Orleans Fire, rebuilt, and then again damaged by fire in 1988 when the entire third floor was destroyed. Six years after the 1988 fire, the Cabildo reopened only to weather Mother Nature again during Hurricane Katrina. The Cabildo is a National Historic Landmark. It now houses some of the best artifacts from around the time of the Louisiana Purchase.

> Roger took Dora to the Cabildo when she was a little girl. MD

> Talamasca members Aaron Lightner and Mary took a young Merrick Mayfair to various museums. The Cabildo is most likely one of the museums Merrick visited. MR

> The Cabildo was used as background in the movie Interview with the Vampire. Movie

Directions 9

Caddy corner to the Cabildo are the Upper Pontalba Apartments.

Upper Pontalba Apartments

The night before Lestat met with Raglan James, the body thief, Louis found Lestat in the Cathedral. After Louis express his concerns about the body switch, Lestat saw him leave near the Upper Pontalba Apartments. BT

Directions 10

Walk down St. Peter Street, away from the church and towards the front entrance of Jackson Square, which is Decatur Street. When you get to Decatur Street, stop. Take a look at the building across the street to your right, 620 Decatur Street, Jackson Brewing Company, also known as JAX Brewery. This building has commercial space on the bottom floors and luxury condos on the upper floors.

Jackson Brewery

Jax Brewery was originally the Socola Rice Mill, and later became the Jackson Brewery Millhouse building. Angelo Socola, an Italian immigrant, owned the rice mill. The original building was designed and constructed by German-born and -educated architect Dietrich Einsiedel in 1891. After a series of lawsuits and other legal problems, Socola Rice Mill became a brewery. During Prohibition from 1919 to about 1933, Jax Brewery stopped brewing alcohol and began bottling other types of brews. Once Prohibition was lifted, Jax Brewery went back to brewing and bottling beer, becoming one of the largest independent breweries in the South.

Unfortunately, Jax Brewery could not compete with national beer companies. After years of declining sales, they were forced into bankruptcy. The building was abandoned for several years. In the early 1980s, the building was purchased by investors and turned into space for shops, restaurants, and perhaps the most luxurious condos in the French Quarter. The restored building opened in 1984.

> There are at least two luxury penthouses in Jax Brewery, and based on Lestat's description, it's almost certain that he owned one prior to restoring his Royal Street home. Lestat describes his penthouse as, "My little rooftop apartment in the French Quarter, which for all its glamour is not very high at all, being on the top of a four-storey building, erected long before the Civil War, and having a rather intimate view of the river and its beautiful twin bridges, and which catches, when the windows are open, the noises of the happily crowded Cafe du Monde and of the busy shops and streets around Jackson Square."
>
> Note, since Lestat owned his penthouse the building has been remodeled and looks a little (not much) different today. BT

> Lestat stopped by his rooftop flat to put on a heavy wool overcoat, proud of his newly bronzed skin, before he went to Jackson Square to meet Raglan James for the first time. BT

Talamasca members would spy on Lestat from Café du Monde. At the time Lestat owned his penthouse, there were not as many trees blocking the view like you see today. Therefore, the Talamasca members had a clear view of Lestat's rooftop flat or penthouse. BT

The penthouse patio is approximately 800 square feet. Lestat used part of patio for his rooftop garden. BT

Directions 11

When it's safe to do so, cross Decatur Street and walk to rear of Jax Brewery. Look upriver, to your right, and you will see the beautiful twin bridges Lestat calls his Dixie Gates.

Dixie Gates

The two bridges you see up-river are known by many names, Greater New Orleans (GNO) Bridge, the Crescent City Connection, twin river bridges, Dixie Gates. They are called twin cantilever (meet in the middle) bridges.

The cantilever bridges were designed by Modjeski & Masters. Construction began on the first bridge, (than known as the Greater New Orleans (GNO) Bridge in November 1954. The Bridge opened for traffic in April 1958. Construction on the second bridge began in March 1981. The second bridge opened for traffic in September 1988. The bridges are ranked as the fifth most traveled toll bridges in the United States. Each bridge has four general-use automobile lanes.

> Lestat speaks of his "Dixie Gates" at least three times throughout the vampire chronicles. He would roam

up and down the riverfront area, close to his Dixie Gates, just to kick around cans and think. Lestat loved the bridge's twinkling lights. His favorite spot was the empty field close to the wharves, stretching beneath the giant pylons of the freeways. IV and BT

▸ If you take the free ferry ride cross the Mississippi River, you will get a great look at Lestat's Dixie Gates. IV and BT

Directions 12

Turn around and head towards the small park next to Jackson Brewery. Walk up the ramp or stairs leading to main lookout area of the park. This is the Washington Artillery Park.

Washington Artillery Park

On and near this site since 1718 has centered the military activities of both regular and citizen soldiers of France, Spain, the Confederacy and the United States. On either side were the redoubts forming the "Great Battery" which crisscrossed its fires with those of Fort San Carlos (Ft. St. Charles) at the foot of Esplanade Avenue and Fort San Luis (Ft. St. Louis) at the river end of Canal Street. One block down river is the lot used as an artillery park for Spanish, French and American cannons. From here and from Place Darmer across the street the cannoniers, bombardiers of France, the Royal Artillery of Spain, the Battalion D'Artillerie D'Orleans, and for the last 100 years, the Washington Artillery (141st Field Artillery) have fired the salutes welcoming distinguished visitors to the Crescent City. To them and to they're worthy successors this park is dedicated.

> ▶ This is the river lookout opposite Jackson Square that Michael and Rowan visited when they spent time roaming the French Quarter. WH

Directions 13

Next to the Washington Artillery Park is Café du Monde. Make your way down the ramp and walk over to the Café.

Café du Monde

Café du Monde is where the old French Market officially began. The first building in the French Market was called the Halle des Boucheries, or the "Butcher's Market." The only things sold were fresh fish and meat. By the mid-1800s, vendors begin to move out of the French Market and into the local neighborhoods. Stalls became available to new vendors. Fred Koeniger opened Café Du Monde around 1862. It was a traditional coffee shop serving his family's recipe for a tasty pastry called beignets. In the beginning, Koeniger's coffee shop consisted of small tabletops and sitting stools.

Hubert Fernandez, who had worked for United Fruit Company, went to work in his family business, Fernandez Wine Cellar, located on the ground floor of the Pontalba apartment building. Fernandez became a regular customer and friend to Koeniger. When Koeniger informed Fernandez of his plans for retirement, Fernandez made arrangements to buy Café Du Monde from him. Hubert Fernandez took ownership of the café in 1942 and to this day it is a family operated business. It is the oldest continuous tenant in the French Market.

- Michael Curry and Rowan Mayfair took a break from their romantic stroll to enjoy the famous café au lait and sugared donuts called beignets. WH

- Lestat and Raglan James discussed terms of the body switch here. BT

- Talamasca members would sit in the café and spy on Lestat and his penthouse. BT

- Lestat found himself sitting in the Café du Monde in a mortal body trying to figure out how to break into his luxurious rooftop rooms. Lestat had fitted the entry to the roof garden with an impassable iron gate. He also secured the doors of the penthouse itself with numerous and complex locks. BT

Directions 14

Go ahead and meander through the French Market shops behind Café Du Monde just as Yuri, a Talamasca member, did on his way to see Aaron Lightner at Beatrice Mayfair home on Esplanade Avenue. When you get to 923 Decatur Street, Central Grocery Company, stop.

Central Grocery Company

Since 1906 they have served Italian, French, Spanish and Greek Specialties. Central Grocery is famous for their Muffuletta sandwiches, and claims to be "Home of the Original Muffuletta."

Salvatore Lupo, a Sicilian immigrant, founded Central Grocery in 1906 and made it a small, old-fashioned Italian-American grocery store. The grocery store has retained much of its old-world-market feel. It's a little dark and a little dusty. The tasty sandwich was created to feed the Sicilian immigrants who worked or sold goods in the French Market. A Muffuletta is a circular (about 10 inches across) loaf of Italian bread, piled with Italian salami and ham, provolone cheese, and an awesome yummy salad of chopped green and black olives, along with anchovies, garlic, and other secret ingredients. You can buy a whole or half sandwich.

Central Grocery's Muffuletta has been featured on many television shows as one of the top five or top ten sandwiches in the world. They also sell their famous sandwich and olive salad fixings via mail order. Grab a Muffuletta and a soda for when you take a break later if you like.

> One of Roger's happiest memories was the time he took Dora, by taxi, to the French Quarter for a Muffuletta from Central Grocery. MD

Directions 15

From Central Grocery continue down Decatur Street.

Tidbit - Stella Mayfair

Look at the buildings to your right and left. You will see a mixture of commercial and residential buildings. Stella Mayfair, who wanted privacy, bought a building on Decatur Street, which was to be used as a studio. This is most likely the area Stella bought her building. WH

> ▸ Stella and Ancient Evelyn became lovers on a trip to Europe and the affair continued when they came home. Stella found an enchanting little courtyard apartment just for her and Ancient Evelyn in the French Quarter. LS

Directions 16

Continue to meander in the French Market until you get to Decatur and Ursulines Streets. If you have not crossed the street yet, cross the street and head over to the market you see to your right. The small, short street next to the French Market is French Market Place. This short street was once known as the infamous Gallatin Street.

Gallatin Street

Gallatin Street was a short alley that ran from the French Market to the Mint. It is named after Abraham Alfonse Albert Gallatin, Secretary of the Treasury under Jefferson and Madison. The infamous Gallatin Street was the first red-light district in New Orleans, and the place where jazz began. No longer in existence, Gallatin Street, which existed from 1840 to 1875, was officially changed to French Market Place on August 7, 1935. There were many who never made it past those short blocks alive. Prostitution, gambling, sodomy, rape, molestation, indecent exposure, and other forcible sexual acts, along with aggravated assault, manslaughter, and murder were considered business as usual on Gallatin Street.

It's rumored that pirates would kidnap victims and force them to work on their ship with severe punishment as their only pay.

Slaves (on their off days) and free men of color would gather to play music in Congo Square. A Gallatin Street bar owner invited them to come play in his bar. Patrons loved the racy lyrics and music. The music became known as jazz. More and more Gallatin street bar owners invited Congo Square musicians to come play in their establishments. When the red-light district moved from Gallatin Street to Storyville, so did jazz music. By the 1930s, jazz had become popular across all color lines. Today Gallatin Street is mostly restaurants, stores and storage. Go over and take a walk through the new French Market.

- Lestat and Louis went arm and arm to hunt on Gallatin Street and the riverfront taverns. IV

- Lestat and Louis rented rooms on the riverfront. IV

- Julien dressed Katherine, Mary Beth, and Stella as young men and took them to the seedy parts of the French Quarter such as Storyville, Gallatin Street, and other riverfront bars and clubs. Katherine dressed up as a young sailor, with a bandage on her head to cover up her hair. WH

Directions 17

When you are finished exploring Gallatin Street, go over and take a walk through the French Market.

French Market

The French Market began as a Native American trading post for the Choctaw Indians before 1718. Throughout the years, the land now known as the French Market has gone from being an Indian trading post, to the infamous Gallatin Street, to being an open-air market. The market was destroyed by a hurricane and rebuilt. The French Market District was established around 1791. In 1932, the Public Works Administration (PWA) set out to change the image of the area. They changed Gallatin Street's name to French Market Place, remodeled the sheds and stalls, and updated the electrical system. The end results were outstanding.

One interesting fact about the French Market is that it can be traced back to 1870, when a structure with the name the

"Bazaar Market" was built. The structure was considered a functional, well-lit building, which was unusual for its time. However, what is most significant was its designer, a man named Joseph Abeilard, one of the country's first African-American architects.

> When Lestat returned to New Orleans in Tales of the Body Thief with his dog, Mojo, he stopped by a restaurant opposite the French Market and bought Mojo a mess of bones. BT

> Lestat walks Mojo through French Quarter. Lestat would take Mojo walking through the narrow streets of the French Quarter. He would laugh to myself at how mortals stared at Mojo, and gave him a wide berth and seemed indeed to be terrified of Mojo, when he was the one to fear. BT

> When Lestat returned to New Orleans after reclaiming his body from the body thief, he let Louis see me near the old French Market with. Lestat gave Louis a little wink to let him know it was truly Lestat whom he saw. BT

Directions 18

Continue to meander in the market until you get to the end of the French Market. You are behind the old Mint. Turn right and walk to the corner of Barracks Street and cross the street when it is safe. Continue walking until you get to the corner of Esplanade Avenue and N. Peters Street. Look to your right and you will see Esplanade Avenue and Governor Nicholls Wharfs.

Govenor Nicholls & Esplanade Wharfs

Before the beautification of the riverfront, these type of wharfs, many much much bigger dominated the Mississippi riverfront. A wharf is a large area where ships can tie-up and load or unload. The word wharf comes from the Old English hwearf, meaning "bank" or "shore", and its plural is either wharfs or wharves. It is also an acronym for warehouse at riverfront.

- Michael Curry's grandfather worked as a policeman on the wharves, where his father had once loaded cotton bales. WH

- Michael would go to the wharf to see the famous banana boats. The cotton and banana warehouse were once located under the Crescent City Connection aka Dixie Gates. WH

Directions 19

Turn left on Esplanade Avenue and begin walking down the avenue. The area on your left was once Fort St. Charles and later The New Orleans Mint. If you like to learn more about both, be sure to take our French Quarter tour.

Esplanade Avenue

Esplanade is a French word for a flat, level, or open stretch of land, be it grassy, dirt, or paved. An Esplanade is usually found along a body of water, lake, river, or sea. In the early days the Esplanade was a key military area. When New Orleans was originally settled, soldiers used the area for drills and parades. It was customary, as it is today, to call a place by its final destination. The French called the final destination Esplanade. People, mainly men, brought to New Orleans to join the Royal Army, referred to the passage to military camp/training the Esplanade passage. The passage was located on an important portage route between the Bayou and Lake Pontchartrain leading to the Mississippi River. The passage was also a convenient spot for local tradesmen. The Esplanade passage became Esplanade Road and finally Esplanade Avenue.

When the Civil War was over and the military moved out, wealthy French Creoles who did not want to mix with the Americans settled in the area. The French Creoles built exquisite ornate mansions on the street now known as Esplanade Avenue.

> Descendants of Suzette, Lestan, Maurice, and other French Mayfair's lived in picturesque homes on Esplanade Avenue. WH

> Lauren Mayfair, who gave Michael and Rowan an engagement party, lived on Esplanade Avenue. WH

> Beatrice Mayfair, who later married Aaron Lightner of the Talamasca, lived on Esplanade Avenue. WH

- Lionel Mayfair appeared at Mass with one of the downtown cousins who lived in a beautiful old house on Esplanade Avenue. WH

- Claire Mayfair and her family lived in a beautiful old house on Esplanade Avenue. WH

- Mona Mayfair bought barbecue from a decrepit restaurant on Esplanade Street just outside the French Quarter because she liked the smell. LR

- Edith Mayfair bled to death alone in her apartment on Esplanade Avenue after Lasher attempted to mate with her. LR

- Yuri, with men following him, meets Aaron at Beatrice Mayfair house on Esplanade Avenue. LR

- Patsy Blackwood conceived Quinn Blackwood in a home on Esplanade Avenue. BF

Directions 20

Continue walking on Esplanade Avenue until you get to the corner of Esplanade Avenue and Decatur Street. Turn right and look across the street. The neighborhood across the street from the French Quarter is Faubourg Marigny.

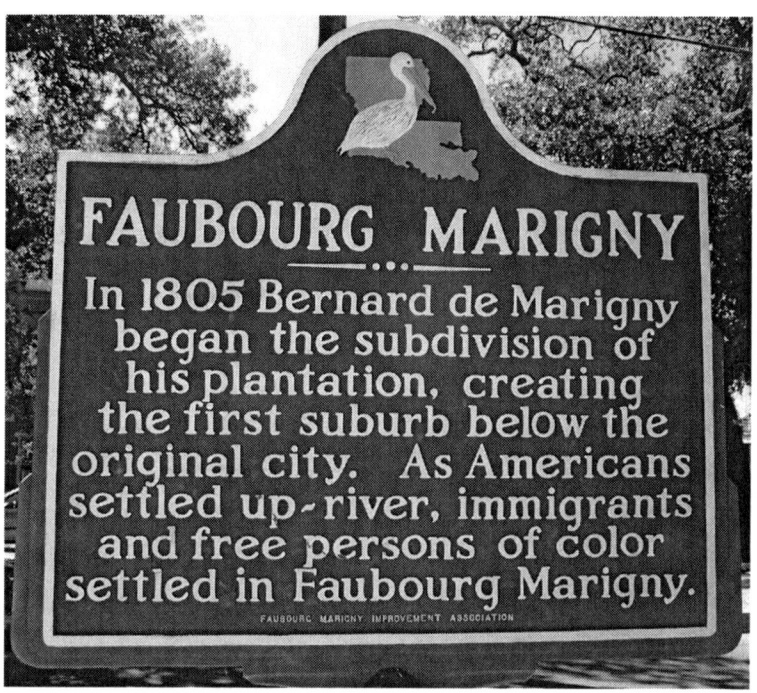

Faubourg Marigny

Records relating to the property, which are in French, include an act of April 19, 1805, allowing Bernard de Marigny to divide his plantation into lots and offer them for sale. This neighborhood was developed by plantation owner and eccentric millionaire Bernard de Marigny de Mandeville in the early 1800s. Its borders are odd due to the bend of the Mississippi River. The Marigny was the third village or municipality to be incorporated into New Orleans. In the early 1800s, white gentlemen often kept their colored mistresses and the children born to them in the Marigny.

Unfortunately, the stately Marigny neighborhood experienced a decline in the mid-1900s and became a hotbed of crime and vice. In the late 1900s, the neighborhood experienced a rebirth when the 1984 World's Fair came to town. Known for its live music and restaurants, it is now a popular and revitalized tourist spot.

> When Louis and Claudia were making arrangements to leave Lestat, Louis made plans to leave Lestat an income which would guarantee Lestat could continue to live the life he was accustomed to and buy their freedom at the same time. One of the businesses Louis planned to leave Lestat was a small construction company located in the Faubourg Marigny. IV

> After Lestat got his body back, he passed through the Faubourg Marigny to get to the swamplands, where he took to the clouds to revisit Georgetown and the young woman his mortal self had so unforgivably raped. BT

Directions 21

Continue walking down Esplanade Avenue until you get to Chartres Street. Turn left onto Chartres Street and continue walking until you get to Governor Nicholls Street.

Tidbit - Talamasca

Erich Stool and two or three other men from the Talamasca's Order followed Yuri when he walked up Chartres Street after leaving Beatrice Mayfair home on Esplanade Avenue. LR

Directions 22

At Chartres and Governor Nicholls Street turn right and continue until you get to the corner of Royal Street.

Bayou Road

Native Americans, the first settlers, used the bayou trail or path as a way of getting to and from the lake to the Mississippi River. This route became known as Bayou Road. When the new settlers established a formal path they called it Rue de l'Arsenal Street until approximately 1729. It was later known as Rue de l'Hôpital because the King's Hospital, or the Royal Hospital, was the last destination on this street. The street was renamed Governor Nicholls Street on October 6, 1909, to honor Francis Tillou Nicholls, twice governor of the state. Bayou Road exists today as an extension of Governor Nicholls Street starting at Claiborne Avenue.

▸ When Lestat and Louis moved to the French Quarter, Bayou Road was one of the main paths leading to New Orleans. IV

▸ Families used Bayou Road to come into New Orleans for the theatre, opera, balls, the social season, or to shop. IV

▸ Claudia and Louis most likely took Lestat's body by carriage down Royal Street to Bayou Road/Governor Nicholls Street, turned left on Bayou Road and continued down this road to the swamp, where they left his remains. IV

Tidbit - Mandy Mayfair

Mandy Mayfair, the third female in the Mayfair family to die when Lasher attempted to mate with her lived in the French Quarter.

Directions 23

Continue until you get to the corner of Royal and Governor Nicholls Streets, turn right and walk until you get to 1132 Royal Street, Gallier House.

Gallier House

On May 19, 1857, James Gallier, Jr. purchased this lot, which was part of the Ursuline Convent grounds from 1727 until 1825. Gallier, Jr. designed and built this residence in 1857, adding additions in 1860. Gallier and his father were the leading New Orleans architects who designed the old French Opera House, the original St. Charles Exchange Hotel, Municipality Hall (now Gallier Hall), and the Pontalba Apartment Buildings. The family name in Ireland was Gallagher, but they changed it to Gallier when they immigrated to New Orleans.

Gallier, his wife, and their four daughters lived in this house until his death in 1868, after which his widow and children lived here until 1917. The townhouse contains an early working bathroom, a passive ventilation system, and furnishings of the period. Gallier followed the fashion of the day by using Trompe l'oeil techniques to create the impression of exterior granite blocks on the plastered brick façade and the look of marble and beautifully grained wood in the interior. The color of the balcony, known as "Paris green," was meant to simulate the patina of oxidized copper or bronze. The house was declared a National Historic Landmark on February 15, 1974.

- Anne Rice used the Gallier House as a model for Lestat, Louis, and Claudia's fictional Rue Royale (Royal Street) home. The vampires lived in this house from 1795 to 1862, over 65 years. IV

- Jesse Reeves comes to New Orleans at the behest of the Talamasca, to investigate Louis's account of the events in the townhouse. QD

- Lestat restored the townhouse and brought his dog, Mojo, to live with him. BT

- Louis attempted to kill himself in the rear courtyard. MR

- Lestat fed Louis blood and made him a stronger vampire here. MK

- Louis made Merrick a vampire here. MK

Directions 24

Continue to walk down Royal Street until you get to Ursulines Street. Turn left and walk one block to Chartres Street. Turn left at Ursulines Avenue and Chartres Streets. Walk until you get to 1112 Chartres Street, Old Ursuline Convent.

Old Ursuline Convent

This is one of the oldest remaining French colonial buildings from the original colony. The Ursuline Sisters came to New Orleans in 1727. Without them, this city would have been a very different place. The nuns provided the first decent medical care for non-military colonists, poor, slaves, and Indians. They established the country's first all-girl school, orphanages, and asylums. They set up schools for the children of the colonists, as well as for the slaves and Native Americans. They helped raise girls shipped over from France as marriage material for local men, teaching the girls everything from languages to homemaking and personal care. The Sisters are credited with establishing the city's first Charity Hospital and the oldest school in America.

The Ursuline Convent that you see today is on a very small portion of the land of the original convent. Some of the land was sold to raise money. Due to hurricanes and fire, part of the convent was condemned and never rebuilt. The convent's girl's school, which was founded in 1727, moved uptown in the 1800s. The old convent was declared a National Historic Landmark on October 15, 1966.

> ▸ Louis found Claudia near Ursuline Convent. Claudia informed Louis she wanted her own coffin. IV

> ▸ Both, Deirdre and Stella Mayfair were expelled from Ursuline Academy. WH

Directions 25

Walk back towards Ursulines Street, and continue until you get to Chartres and Dumaine Streets.

Condé Street Ballroom

The street we now know as Chartres Street was called Condé Street between Esplanade Avenue and Orleans Street. The Condé Street Ballroom was located between Chartres and Dumaine Streets. The simple wooden ballroom catered to "whites only". The main attractions were some of the most beautiful Quadroon women to be found anywhere in the city. A quadroon is a person who has one-quarter black ancestry. The mixture is often associated with someone of black and European ancestry. Prominent men of the city who were looking for a mistress usually attended the balls.

▶ On the night Louis let Lestat lead him out of the St. Louis Hotel and down the back stairs to the hospital they found Claudia alive, they saw people coming from the Condé Street ballroom. IV

Tidbit - Dumaine Street

Dumaine Street, which was at one time an extremely fashionable street, shows up in Anne's novels a lot.

▶ Lestat's musician friend lived on Dumaine Street. IV

▶ Lestat and Louis attended a music recital at Madame LeClair, who also lived Dumaine Street. IV

▶ Louis and Lestat owned property on Dumaine Street. VC

▶ Upon arrival in New Orleans, Marie Claudette moved her family into a large house in the Rue Dumaine, and immediately acquired an enormous plantation at Riverbend, south of the city. WH

▶ Julien bought a townhouse on Dumaine Street from Darcy Monahan, Katherine's husband. WH & LR

Directions 26

Go back in the directions you just came and continue to walk down Chartres Street until you come to 823 Chartres Street, Librairie Bookshop.

Librairie Book Shop

The owner, Carey Beckham once worked for S.D. Siler Book Company (Samuel Dean), which opened around 1915. Carey Beckham opened Librairie Bookshop at 811 Royal Street in 1967. He had a hard time making ends meet selling new books. He began selling used books and was very successful. He moved his bookstore to Chartres Street in 1985. Librairie Bookstore is the oldest antiquarian and second-hand bookstore, open for over forty-five years, in the French Quarter.

> Mary Beth Mayfair purchased Richard Llewellyn a building that would have been setup much like this Bookstore. Richard's bookstore would be on the ground floor and living quarters on the upper floors. This building is around the corner from Julien's townhouse on Dumaine Street. WH

Directions 27

Walk back towards the direction you just came and stop at the corner of Chartres and Dumaine Streets.

Tidbit - Voodoo Occult Shops

Dumaine Street was once the most popular street in the French Quarter to buy voodoo, occult and similar supplies.

Just a few feet to the right and left on Dumaine Street are two occult/voodoo shops. Esoterica Occult Goods is at 541 Dumaine Street and Voodoo Authentica is at 612 Dumaine Street. If you'd like to stop and take a look at these shops, go ahead. We will be here when you are ready. We suggest you visit Esoterica first because your tour will pick up on Dumaine Street close to Voodoo Authentica.

Directions 28

If you did not visit the occult and voodoo stores, at Chartres and Dumaine Streets, turn left on Dumaine Street and walk until you get to 632 Dumaine Street, Madame John's Legacy.

If you visited Esoterica Occult Goods at 541 Dumaine Street, when you leave the shop turn right and walk toward Chartres Street to Voodoo Authentica and Madame John's Legacy.

If you are leaving Voodoo Authentica, 612 Dumaine Street, turn left after you walk out of the shop and walk to 632 Dumaine Street, Madame John's Legacy.

Madame John's Legacy

This is one of the oldest buildings in the French Quarter (Ursuline Convent is the other one). Records show the house was originally erected in 1726, eight years after the founding of New Orleans. Natchez Indians killed the first owner, Jean Pascal, a sea captain from Provence, France, who came to New Orleans on January 15, 1726. Engineer-architect Ignace Francois Broutin's map of the city from 1728 shows Captain Pascal's land on lot 92, and here it was that the mariner, his wife, and daughter lived. The fire of 1788 destroyed portions of the original structure. The parts of the original building that survived the fire were used in its reconstruction in 1789. The building you see now is very close to an exact replica of the original house.

Stella Hirsch Lemann purchased the house in 1925 and happily saw to its preservation. The home remained in her possession until 1947, when she donated the house to the Louisiana State Museum. The name "Madame John's Legacy" is from George Washington Cable's book Old Creole Days. The house was willed to the main character, a quadroon and free woman of color named Madame John. The house was declared a National Historic Landmark on April 15, 1970.

> The house can be seen in the movie Interview with the Vampire. Brad Pitt's voice-over narrates the scene as men carry caskets down the stairs to waiting horse-drawn hearses. IV

> Antha Mayfair, who wanted to be a writer, would go to the French Quarter to try to get the poets and writers to pay attention to her work. WH

Tidbit - Marguerite Mayfair Husband

Marguerite's Mayfair husband, Tyrone Clifford McNamara, cheated on her with a mistress he kept in the French Quarter. For reasons unknown, the house they shared burned down. Her husband and his mistress were both found dead, overcome by smoke trying to escape.

Directions 29

Continue walking down Dumaine Street until you get to the intersection of Dumaine and Royal Streets. Turn left, walk to the middle of the block, and stop.

700 - 900 Rue Royal

You are standing in the middle of the three street blocks used in the film "Interview with the Vampire". Royal Street was completely shut down when the movie "Interview With The Vampire" was filmed in New Orleans in the fall of 1993. The 700 - 900 blocks of Royal Street were converted into an exceptional replica of 17th and 18th century New Orleans. The paved streets were covered with dirt and many of the French Quarter homes and businesses exteriors were used in the film.

Directions 30

Continue walking down Royal Street until you get to St. Ann Street.

Tidbit - St Ann Street

David Talbot and Merrick Mayfair met for the first time after twenty years in a cafe on St. Ann Street. MR

Lestat walked with Louis to St. Louis Cemetery to visit his grave via St. Ann Street. QD

Directions 31

Continue walking down Royal Street until you get to Orleans Street. Turn right and stop at 717 Orleans Street. The large hotel you see to your right was once the Theatre d'Orleans and Orleans Ballroom.

Theatre d'Orleans

Once the edifice where much of the city's cultural exhibitions took place was the Theatre d'Orleans. Although the final incarnation of the building burned down in 1919, this pivotal locale was first established in 1809. When the first structure burned down in 1813, another theatre was built on the same site. The exterior was said to be extremely plain, but the interior was another story. From the crystal chandeliers to the costly dance floor made of three layers of cypress topped with quarter sawn oak, the ballroom was best known as the site for the Balls du Cordon Bleu, otherwise known as the Quadroon Balls. In addition to being a theatre and ballroom, it was the first gambling parlor and functioned as a state house, legislative hall, district court, popular meeting place for the renowned Mardi Gras Krewes, and a restaurant. The glory days ended when the St. Louis Hotel opened a grander ballroom.

The site later became the home of a convent, orphanage, and school for the Sisters of the Holy Family. This was a religious community of black nuns, founded in New Orleans in 1842 by Miss Henriette Delille, a free woman of color and the daughter of a quadroon. They converted the old ballroom into their chapel. The Sisters first opened St. Mary's School (later called St. Mary's Academy) on Chartres Street in 1867. The Sisters sold the theatre in 1964 to a developer, but stayed at the Orleans Avenue location until 1965. Today, the site is the Bourbon Orleans Hotel. The hotel incorporated the façade and other parts of the original building into the hotel's design. The ballroom from 1819 is still part of the building and the hotel is reported to be haunted.

> Henriette Delille is the first native-born American whose cause for canonization has been officially opened by the Catholic Church.

> Lestat, Louis, and Claudia attended events at the Theatre d'Orleans and had their own private box. IV

- The Mayfair's attended events at the various theatres on this site and had their own private box. WH
- Katherine Mayfair, wanting to see the famous quadroon balls had herself presented as a quadroon at one of the balls. Julien fought at least one duel over this prank. WH

Tidbit - Julien Mayfair

- Julien took Mary Beth to the opera and treated her as his niece, showering her with attention.
- According to Richard Llewellyn, one of Julien's antics was dressing his male lover's up as a woman and taking him to the opera. They fooled everyone and no one ever had the slightest suspicion.

Directions 32

Continue walking until you get to 730 Orleans Street, Crescent City Cigar Shop, opposite side of the street.

Crescent City Cigar Shop

The Crescent City Cigar Shop was established in 1998 by Armando Ortiz, a cigar lover and very friendly man. In Armando's cigar shop you can find premium and international cigars that other shops have never heard about. They have one of the largest walk-in humidors New Orleans. Armando will take time to answer any questions you have about cigars. If he does not carry the cigar you want, he will go out of his way to get it for you. This includes Rothmans cigarettes.

Rothmans International PLC was a British tobacco manufacturer founded by Louis Rothman in 1890. By the 1900s Rothman opened a small store on Pall Mall Street in London. Pall Mall Street is best known for the gentlemen's clubs built in the 19th and early 20th centuries. By 1929

Rothmans was listed on the London Stock Exchange, and was at one time a constituent of the FTSE 100 Index. After a series of acquisitions and mergers, Rothmans was acquired by British American Tobacco PLC in 1999. The brand is not popular in the United States. Rothmans are often used in the voodoo community and sold in some voodoo shops. Crescent City Cigar Shop sells Rothmans Cigarettes. If they don't have them in stock, they can get them.

> ▸ Matthew Kemp, the man Merrick wished had been her father and referred to as her stepfather, went to the French Quarter to buy Rothmans, his favorite cigarettes. MK

Directions 33

Continue walking until you get to the corner of Orleans Avenue and Bourbon Street.

Bourbon Street

Bourbon Street is one of the original streets of New Orleans. The street is named after the House of Bourbon, one of the ruling royal houses of France. Bourbon Street was a premier residential area prior to 1900. Many of the commercial establishments moved into the area when the red-light district moved to Storyville, which was adjacent to the French Quarter.

> One of Lestat's favorite hunting places was Bourbon Street, where he could find one or two good meals for the night, or someone from which he could take a little drink. IV

> Stella and Stuart Townsend talked early into the following morning at a speakeasy on Bourbon Street after a more respectable place had kicked them out. WH

Tidbit - French Quarter

> According to Richard Llewellyn, Julien took Lionel and Stella, dress like a little sailor boy, with him to the French Quarter to see the unseemly sights. WH

> Julien and Mary Beth hired dance bands from the Quarter. WH

Directions 34

Turn left onto Bourbon Street and walk until you get to St. Peter Street. Turn left again and walk until you get to 723-25 St. Peter Street, Reverend Zombie's House of Voodoo and Cigar Shop.

Tidbit - Reverend Zombie's

This is another example of a voodoo store in New Orleans.

> When you walk through the front door, look towards the ceiling, you will see a pair of iron gates. They are movie memorabilia (props) from the movie, "Interview with the Vampire".

Directions 35

Continue down St. Peter Street until you get to Royal Street. Turn right on Royal Street and walk until you get to 613 Royal Street, Court of Two Sisters.

Court of Two Sisters

It is said that Sieur Etienne de Perier, Royal Governor of Colonial Louisiana between 1726 and 1733, was the original owner of this property. The original structure was destroyed by the Great New Orleans Fire of 1788. A private residence was built on the property in 1832. Antoine Cavalier acquired the residence and made it his home and mercantile establishment for many years. When he died, he passed it on to his sons, Antoine Jr. and Zenon, who also had a mercantile business. Eventually, two sisters, Emma and Bertha Camors, acquired the property and opened a notions and variety store. The sisters began outfitting many of the city's finest women with formal gowns, lace, and perfumes imported from Paris. They operated their store for over twenty years, from 1886 to 1906. Marriage, reversals of fortune, widowhood—nothing could separate the two sisters. The sisters died two months apart in the winter of 1944. United in death as in life, the sisters lie side by side at St. Louis Cemetery #3. After their deaths, the ownership and use of the property changed hands many times before it became a restaurant. Its deep, handsome courtyard was made famous by the many pictorial reproductions made of it.

- Stella Mayfair took Stuart Townsend, Talamasca member, to the Court of Two Sisters. WH
- Richard Llewellyn had lunch with Stella Mayfair at the Court of Two Sisters. WH

Tidbit - Royal Street

- Michael and Rowan browse the shops on Royal Street on their romantic walk. WH
- The Old Captain sold books and things through a shop on Royal Street. MD

Directions 36

Continue walking until you get to the corner of Royal and Toulouse Streets. Turn right. Walk until you get to Bourbon Street. The large hotel across the street on your left, 541 Bourbon Street, was once the location of the French Opera House.

French Opera House

The French Opera House was designed by James Gallier, and erected in 1859. It was once the tallest building in the French Quarter. The original building featured an elliptical auditorium that could accommodate 1,800 people over four tiered levels. The fourth tier was for colored, Indians, servants, and other lesser patrons. The Opera House also had sections for those wishing privacy such as ladies in mourning, madams from Storyville, pregnant ladies, and married men with their mistresses.

Most of the performances were in French. Monday through Saturday were considered the "respectful performances." On Sundays, a completely different troupe would perform more risqué performances. Many patrons could be heard singing or humming the songs from the opera on the street or at home. The French Opera House hosted many social events, including carnival balls. In 1919, the French Opera House burned clear to the ground, saving very little of its notable past. Another Opera House was built on this spot and it too burned down, never to be rebuilt. The land was donated to Tulane University. Over the years, the land was used for many different establishments before becoming the Inn On Bourbon Ramada Plaza Hotel.

- Lestat, Louis, and Claudia would watch shows from a private box when they went to the opera. IV

- Marguerite Mayfair and family watched the opera from a private box.

- Planters would come into the city with their families to go to the French Opera House. The farmer would sit in one of the lower three tiers and their servants would sit on the fourth tier. IV

- Several witnesses mention Marguerite's mysterious dark-haired lover, seen in her box at the French Opera House.

Directions 37

Walk up Bourbon Street until you get to St. Louis Street. Turn right on St. Louis and walk until you get to 820 Saint Louis Street, Hermann-Grima House.

Hermann-Grima House

This Federal-style mansion, built in 1831, was home to prosperous Creole families. Samuel Hermann, Sr., a wealthy commission merchant, built the home, which stretched from St. Louis Street to Conti Street, soon after he purchased the land on May 19, 1823. American architect William Brand completed the house. The mansion remained the home of the Hermanns until 1844 when, owing to financial difficulties, it was then sold to Felix Grima, a noted attorney and notary. The home remained in the Grima family through the rigors of the Civil War before becoming a boarding house in the 1920s. The house was meticulously restored by the Christian Woman's Exchange and is open to the public for tours. It is now a museum, with the only standing horse stable and outside kitchen in the French Quarter.

The house was declared a National Historic Landmark on August 19, 1971.

> Talamasca members Aaron and Mary took Merrick frequently to the local museums. The Hermann-Grima Historic House is most likely one of the museums Merrick visited. MR

Directions 38

At this time, you need to turn around and head back towards Bourbon Street. Continue down St. Louis Street to 713 St. Louis Street, Antoine's Restaurant.

Antoine's Restaurant

Antoine Alciatore moved to New Orleans from New York. He worked in various restaurants in the French Quarter, including the St. Charles Hotel, before opening his own,

Antoine's Restaurant, in 1868. The building was erected as a private residence and had several owners before Antoine purchased it for his restaurant. The original Antoine's Restaurant, called Pension Alciatore, was located one block away. This restaurant outgrew that space and needed a much larger location. Antoine established two sources of income with a boarding house and restaurant, counting on one business to keep the other afloat as he established his restaurant. This arrangement was common in New Orleans for new and established businesses.

With a steady source of income from his rentals and restaurant, Antoine acquired a larger building, and the rest is history. The restaurant is famous for its great food and extensive wine cellar. For many years, Antoine hosted many Mardi Gras Krewes. Only one thing has changed in the restaurant over the years: they no longer cook on French coal ranges because replacement parts became impossible to get. Antoine's is the oldest family-run restaurant in the United States.

> ▹ Cecilia Mayfair's engagement dinner for Rowan and Michael, with a guest list of approximately two hundred family members, was at Antoine's Restaurant. WH

Directions 39

Continue walking down St. Louis Street until you get to Royal Street. Turn left. Stop at 520 Royal Street, WDSU-TV Station.

WDSU-TV Front Entrance

WDSU-TV began broadcasting on Saturday, December 18, 1948. It was the first television station in Louisiana. The middle call letters stand for DeSoto, as in DeSoto Hotel, the first broadcast location. From 1950 until they moved in 1996, the television studio was here, in the Seignouret-Brulatour Mansion.

WDSU's studio is where Dora taped her television show. Lestat kidnapped her in the rear of this building. We will see that location in a few minutes. MD

Directions 40

Turn around and go back to St. Louis Street. Turn left. This building, 621 St. Louis Street, was once the site of the St. Louis Hotel.

St Louis Hotel

This is where the St. Louis Hotel once stood. The first hotel on this site was the City Exchange Hotel, established in 1838 and named after a very famous cafe/coffeehouse/bar and popular meeting place that was already on the site. The Creoles designed the hotel to outdo the Americans' hotel, which was across Canal Street. Over time people began referring to the hotel as the St. Louis Exchange, identifying the hotel with the street name "St. Louis." The hotel was partially destroyed by a fire in 1841. Famed architect Jacques Nicolas Bussière de Pouilly rebuilt the hotel. The hotel's name was changed to the St. Louis Hotel around 1843.

The St. Louis Hotel was one of New Orleans' premier hotels until the Civil War, when the once-grand hotel became a hospital for the Confederate Army. It was completely destroyed by a hurricane in 1915, leaving only a few arches of the edifice. After years of debates about what to do with the property, a new hotel, Royal Orleans, opened on this spot in 1960. Omni International Hotels acquired the hotel and changed its name to the Omni Royal Orleans.

- The St. Louis Hotel is where Lestat and Louis lived when they arrived in New Orleans from Louis Plantation. IV

- Several witnesses mention Marguerite's mysterious dark-haired lover who was seen in her suite at the St Louis Hotel. WH

- Remy, Julien, and Katherine, supervised by only a quadroon governess, stayed in a lavish suite at the St Louis Hotel. WH

- The St. Louis is where Marguerite Mayfair and family stayed in New Orleans. WH

- Daniel McIntyre moved into an extravagant four-room suite in the St. Louis Hotel after his mother died. WH

Directions 41

The hotel expands the complete block, from Royal to Chartres Streets. Continue walking until you get to Chartres Street. At St. Louis and Chartres Streets, turn right and walk until you get to 410 Chartres Street, Second City Criminal Court, Third Precinct Police Station.

Third Precinct Police Station

The history of the land goes back to the ownership by the Marigny de Mandeville family. A house with a separate kitchen in the back of the property sat on the original lot, which was once part of a larger property extending to the corner of Chartres and Conti Streets. In 1915, Edgar A. Christy, who was then serving as City Architect, designed the Beaux Arts–style structure that you see today. The Beaux Arts building initially functioned as the Third District Police Station and once housed the Second City Criminal Courthouse. The building was purchased by the State of Louisiana in 1957 and sat vacant for several years. In 1993, the former courthouse and police station got a new owner and new life. The building was renovated by the Williams Research Center of the

Historic New Orleans Collection, a research facility with public reading rooms (once courtrooms) for researchers.

> A Mayfair relative who was convicted of assault and battery after a drunken brawl in a French Quarter nightclub was fatally shot when he attempted to escape from the jail. It's said he was more scared of Mary Beth Mayfair's disapproval than the criminal courts. WH

Tidbit - Conti Street

Walk to the corner, Chartres and Conti Streets.

> Louis, enraged by Claudia's plan to kill Lestat, wondered the French Quarter until he found himself listening and watching fencers in a salon on Conti Street. IV

Directions 42

Return to Chartres and St. Louis Streets. At St. Louis Street turn right and stop at 535 St. Louis Street.

Quarter Smith

The Quarter Smith's Ken Bowers is one of the premier jewelers in New Orleans. The shop has been a noted fixture of the community since 1994, but its history stems from years of experience. The owner and shop runner, Ken Bowers, has been a goldsmith for over 38 years, buying and distributing gold, diamonds, watches, and precious metals across the country from his French Quarter shop. In fact, this is where the shop's eponymous name emerges: Quarter, as in "French Quarter," and Smith, as in "Goldsmith."

Don't think for a moment that Bowers and the Quarter Smith have their hands only on the business of gold. Their expertise extends to a variety of jewels and precious metals. They convert jewels and metals into rings, earrings, brooches, and chains, in both traditional and contemporary cuts. In fact, one is able to select loose diamonds and gemstones, or even have their family heirlooms cleaned and restored. Bowers' artisan designs and metalworking have caught the eye of everyone he comes in contact with, from passerby traffic to touring celebrities (a list Ken keeps confidential).

> The shop is responsible for the engraved thumb-pieces used by Tom Cruise in the movie Interview with the Vampire. The shop also created the antique opera glasses and crosses for the film. Movie

> When Aunt Queen went to her favorite goldsmith in the French Quarter to get a gold crucifix on a chain for Quinn, she most likely went to the Quarter Smith. BF

Directions 43

Turn around and return to Chartres and St. Louis Streets. At Chartres Street make a right and stop at 514 Chartres Street, Pharmacy Museum.

Pharmacy Museum

Louis Joseph Dufilho, Jr., America's first licensed pharmacist, originally owned this building, called "Pharmacie Dufilho," "La Pharmacie Francaise," or "apothecary shop." Dufilho purchased the lot On June 2, 1822, and construction began very soon after. In 1823, the Pharmacie Dufilho opened on the ground floor. The Creole-style town house doubled as his home and he cultivated the herbs he needed in the interior courtyard. The City of New Orleans, in conjunction with Loyola University, has converted this old structure into a museum housing an old-time pharmacy that opened in 1950.

The museum has beautiful hand-carved rosewood cabinets from Germany. These 1860 cabinets display fine hand-blown antique apothecary bottles, voodoo potions, medicinal herbs, rare patent medicines, "miracle cures and remedies," live leeches, leech jars, "blood-letting" devices, 19th-century trade cards, pharmacopoeias, prescription files, daily journals, and Civil war Surgical instruments and suppository molds, as well as the old glass cosmetics counter and a seamen's medicine chest—the type used on whaling ships and other tools on exhibit.

> Talamasca members Aaron and Mary took Merrick frequently to the local museums. The Pharmacy Museum is most likely one of the museums Merrick visited. MR

Directions 44

Continue on Chartres Street until you get to the one story garage at 535 Chartres Street, opposite side of the street. This was the rear entrance for WDSU-TV. You saw the front entrance on Royal Street a few minutes ago.

WDSU TV Rear Entrance

WDSU-TV began broadcasting on Saturday, December 18, 1948. It was the first television station in Louisiana. The middle call letters stand for DeSoto, as in DeSoto Hotel, the first broadcast location. From 1950 until they moved in 1996, the television studio was in the Realtor Mansion at 520 Royal Street. The main entrance was for the offices of the television station. The WDSU-TV studio back entrance was at 535 Chartres Street. In between the offices and parking lot was a Quonset hut, which was divided into two studios by a huge door. The door could be opened to allow the two studios to merge into one. There used to be a WDSU-TV sign on the Chartres Street garage entrance. The sign has been removed.

> ▷ Lestat, who had been following Dora and knew her schedule, waited for Dora in the doorway of a nearby shop, approached her as she left the television studio, and took her to New York City by air. MD

Directions 45

Continue walking down Chartres Street until you get to Toulouse Street. Make a right at Toulouse Street and keep walking. Cross Decatur Street at the signal light when it is safe and keep walking until you get to the train tracks. The Toulouse Streetcar stop is to your left. Please watch for the streetcar or trains before crossing to the Woldenberg Riverfront Park.

You are on the Mississippi Riverfront. If you picked up a Muffuletta sandwich and drink from Central Grocery, this is a great time to enjoy them. This is also a great place to rest, take a cruise, and have lunch, people watch, or just enjoy the Mississippi River. You also have a great view of Lestat's Dixie Gates. The walkway you see on your right and left is the Moonwalk.

Moonwalk

The Moonwalk was named in honor of Maurice Edwin "Moon" Landrieu, the mayor of New Orleans from 1970-1978. For most of the city's history, the Riverfront was dedicated to commerce and industry. In 1976 under the Landrieu administration, the Moonwalk was constructed, replacing a cargo wharf and shed that occupied the site. It represented the first step in the city's efforts to reclaim the Riverfront for the enjoyment of all its citizens and visitors.

> Michael Curry and Rowan Mayfair took a long walk on the Moonwalk before sitting on a bench on the riverfront and watching the dark glitter of the water and the dancing boats, as they went by.

Lestat, Louis and Claudia would often walk along the riverfront. IV

Directions 46

Next to this park entrance, you will see the ticket booth for the Steamboat Natchez. Depending on the time of day, the Steamboat Natchez may be docked or out on the mighty Mississippi.

Steamboat Natchez

This is the ninth steamer to bear the name Natchez. The first Natchez was built by Captain Thomas Paul Leather in 1845. Leather was a first-rate showman in every way, and his audiences showed their love for his flamboyant ways by paying good money to ride his steamboat when they traveled. Every Natchez built after the first one was larger than the last. It was Natchez VI that raced Captain John W. Cannon's steamboat, the Robert E. Lee, in the most famous steamboat race of all time. There's a debate as to which boat actually won the race. Some said that the Robert E. Lee won the race because it arrived in St. Louis first. However, the Robert E. Lee did not take on any passengers or cargo. They stripped the ship down to the bare bones and made only one stop. Others said the Natchez won the race because it did not remove anything, and took on passengers and cargo the Robert E. Lee refused to carry.

> The steamboat has had to continuously make arrangements for its calliope player to avoid playing during specific events (such as the St. Louis Cathedral Mass).

> Louis and Claudia departed New Orleans on the French ship Mariana, which was docked on the riverfront. IV

> The Mayfair family traveled between Riverbend and the French Quarter in the early days on a steamboat like the Natchez. WH

> Lestat wondered around "his" Dixie Gates, reminiscing about the fancy steamboats like the Steamboat Natchez. BT

> In the movie Interview with the Vampire, Claudia, Louis, and Lestat strolled along the riverfront and stopped next to a ship, which was a predecessor to the Steamboat Natchez. Movie

Directions 47

When you are ready to continue the tour, walk up the Moonwalk toward the grassy section of the Woldenberg Riverfront Park.

Woldenberg Park

The sixteen acres that start at the Mississippi River and stretch from Audubon Aquarium at Canal Street (upriver) to the Moonwalk in front of Jackson Square (downriver) are known as Woldenberg Riverfront Park. The park is named after its benefactor, local businessman, civic leader, and philanthropist Malcolm Woldenberg. There is a bronze statue of Malcolm Woldenberg in the park.

The area along the Mississippi River became an eyesore with old wharves and abandon warehouses. From the 1970s through the 1980s, many buildings along the riverfront were razed and replaced by Woldenberg Park and the Moonwalk.

Audubon Institute maintains the park. Throughout the year, there are a number of free live music performances, including the French Quarter Festival, boat shows, fireworks, and other activities. Locals and visitors alike enjoy picnics, jogging, or just sitting in the park.

> Michael and Rowan took a long walk on the Moonwalk before sitting on a bench in the Woldenberg Riverfront Park. WH

Directions 48

Take your time and enjoy the sculptures and artwork, many by local artists. Continue down the Moonwalk until you get to Audubon Aquarium of the Americas.

Audubon Aquarium of the Americas

Named in honor of artist and naturalist John James Audubon, Audubon Aquarium is just one part of the Audubon Nature Institute which includes three parks, zoo, aquarium, survival center, theatre, nature center, center for research of endangered species, insectarium, and nature institute. If you want to know anything about nature, you will find someone at the Audubon Institute who can answer your question.

One of the premier aquariums in the country, it is run by the Audubon Institute, the same folks who run the Audubon Zoological Park in the uptown area of the city.

The Aquarium of the Americas is dedicated to the conservation and exploration of the aquatic environments of the Western hemisphere and its adjacent waters through educational and recreational programs. The two-story structure covers 110,000 gross square feet featuring over 7,500 specimens of marine life in more than one million gallons of fresh and salt water.

- Lynelle, Quinn Mayfair's tutor, took Quinn to the Audubon Aquarium. BF

- Aaron and Mary took Merrick into the city frequently to expose her to the splendid museums and galleries. It's highly likely they took her to the Audubon Aquarium during one of those trips. MR

Directions 49

Continue along the walk in front of the Audubon Aquarium and when it's safe, cross the street to the Canal Street-Algiers Ferry. The regular entrance is in the front of the terminal. The handicap/wheelchair entrance is on the right side of the terminal. You can ride the ferry for free.

If you don't want to take a free ferry ride, continue down Canal Street until you get to 365 Canal Street.

Canal Street - Algiers Ferry

The ferry has been the primary form of transportation between New Orleans and Algiers Point for over a hundred years, long before bridges. Algiers was settled in 1719 and it is New Orleans' second oldest neighborhood. New Orleans annexed Algiers in 1870. Algiers Point was once the place African slaves where held before they were sold. A number of slaves came to New Orleans via a slave port name Algiers, and that's the name that stayed with the neighborhood. In the early days, Algiers was not a town, but a private plantation. It was known as Slaughterhouse Point too. Algiers was also the holding area for Cajuns expelled from Nova Scotia.

The ferry began traveling between Jackson Square and Algiers Point in 1827. The ferry can be boarded at the foot of Canal Street, and the trip is free to all pedestrians. You can get off the ferry and meander in the historic Algiers Point. Don't be surprised if you pass the Steamboat Natchez, tugboats pushing enormous barges, or a cruise ship on the Mississippi. Sometimes a dredge boat is visible, dredging the river's silt bottom to keep the channel open for large ships.

Expect the round trip to take from 30-40 minutes. When you return to Canal Street you will depart the ferry and continue down Canal Street.

> Roger took Dora on a ferry ride across the Mississippi. They would sing as they stood by the rail. MD

> As you cross the Mississippi River via ferry, you will get a great look at Lestat's Dixie Gates. IV

> The famous banana boats wharf, which Michael Mayfair went to see, were once located under the Crescent City Connection aka Dixie Gates. You have a great view of the old wharves location from the ferry. WH

Directions 50

Get off the ferry and continue down Canal Street to 365 Canal Street, New Orleans Passport Office. The building is also known as 1 Canal Place.

New Orleans Passport Agency

The New Orleans Passport Agency is a satellite office that assists travelers in the New Orleans area. They can work with you to obtain a US passport in as little as 24 hours. This building is the ninth tallest skyscraper in New Orleans, with thirty-two floors. In the 1720s, a windmill was built on this land. Over the years the river line changed and so did the use of the land. Tradesmen set up stalls in this area and sold goods for many years. By the early 1900s the American Sugar Refinery had a factory on this land. From the 1970s through the 1980s many buildings along the riverfront were razed and the area cleaned up. The sugar refinery moved to Chalmette, Louisiana. The Canal Place project was one of the first major skyscrapers in this area, replacing both the sugar refineries and wharfs. In 1979, the office tower was the first section of the building to be completed. The shops and hotel were completed between 1982-1983.

> In order for Tommy Harrison, Quinn Blackwood's uncle, to get a passport on short notice for their trip to Europe, they had to take Tommy to the Federal Passport Office in New Orleans. It was at this time Quinn changed Tommy's last name from Harrison to Blackwood. Aunt Queen and Quinn vouched that they knew Tommy as Tommy Blackwood. BF

Directions 51

The street pass the Passport Office is N Peters Street. Turn right and continue until you get to 233 N Peters Street, Tipitina's Downtown Hall. Do you recognize the name on top of the building?

Tipitina's

Tipitina's was once an annex location for a famous New Orleans club. The club was named in honor of performer, composer, pianist and founding father of New Orleans R&B, Roy "Professor Longhair" Byrd popular recording, Tipitina.

The title "Professor" gets its origin from Storyville. Every house in Storyville had a piano player who they called a "Professor". Hugh Laurie, from the hit TV Show "House" covered the song in 2011.

Anne Rice's Vampire Fan Club 1997 Coven's Ball was held here.

Directions 52

Facing Tipitina's turn right and walk toward Bienville Street. Turn left onto Bienville Street and walk down to Chartres Street and stop. On the left corner is 241 Chartres Street, former home of Boyer Antiques & Doll Shop.

Boyer Antiques & Doll Shop

For decades, one of New Orleans' famed doll and antique boutiques was the Boyer Antiques Doll and Toy Museum. It was a family-owned-and-operated business specializing in antique dolls and toys dated from the 1800s and early 1900s. Boyer had been at this location since its founding. Here, one could find antique dolls and toys that predated the technology of our modern day, with restored baubles and dolls. Boyer used to be a home to a wide array of finely painted porcelain bisque dolls, created and sold exclusively within Boyer by local artists from all around New Orleans.

Unfortunately, like many of the once-popular local businesses in New Orleans, after Hurricane Katrina, Boyer closed its

BOYER ANTIQUES & DOLL SHOP

business in New Orleans. A gallery of fine photography has replaced this historic business.

Boyer Antiques Doll and Toy Museum Shop was featured in the film adaptation of Interview with the Vampire. This is the shop where Claudia kills the shop owner to get a doll she admired in the window.

> Louis got a bridal doll for Claudia from a doll shop like Boyer's. IV

Directions 53

Continue down Bienville Street until you get to Royal Street. Turn left on Royal Street and walk until you get to 214 Royal Street, Hotel Monteleone.

Hotel Monteleone

The hotel's founder, Antonio Monteleone, owned a successful shoe factory prior to his arrival in America, around 1880. Like many immigrants, Antonio set out to establish himself. To do this, he set up a shoe shop on Royal Street, which was the center of commerce and banking. Customers paid well for Antonio's skilled services. He did so well, he was able to save enough money to invest in a small hotel in 1886 on the corner of Royal and Iberville Streets. From these two businesses, the shoe shop and small hotel, Antonio saved enough money to buy the 64-room Commercial Hotel when it became available. The smaller hotel was incorporated into the Commercial Hotel. In 1908, the combined hotels' names changed to the Hotel Monteleone. This was the beginning of a great family-owned hotel business that reached its 125th birthday in 2011.

For 125 years, the hotel has survived fires, wars, the stock market crash, and the Great Depression. The Hotel Monteleone has had more than its share of famous guests, as well as favorable mentions in television, films, and novels. It's also a favorite destination for ghost hunters. The Hotel Monteleone is a historic landmark and member of Historic Hotels of America.

- Anne and her friend Lucy wrote a threatening note and dropped it on the desk for the Hotel Monteleone staff to locate. When they realized the commotion they caused, they felt bad. Bio

- Aaron Lightner stayed at the Hotel Monteleone when he came to New Orleans for Nancy Mayfair's funeral. WH

- The Old Captain took Roger to lunch and dinner at the Monteleone's restaurant. MD

Directions 54

Walk across the street from Hotel Monteleone at 211 Royal Street is the former home of Hurwitz Mintz Furniture. You can see the store's name in the sidewalk pavement.

Hurwitz Mintz Furniture

When Joseph Hurwitz and Morris Mintz opened a small furniture store on New Orleans' Royal Street in 1923, they had no idea what kind of legacy they had begun. In no time, the store had grown in size and status. It was considered one of the premier mid- to high-end furniture stores in the city. When the second generation took over operations in 1942, Ellis Mintz shepherded the store into an era of great success. The size of the store doubled with a 1963 expansion. After Hurricane Katrina devastated the Crescent City in the fall of 2005, Hurwitz Mintz made the difficult decision to close their French Quarter store on Royal Street.

When Quinn Blackwood drew up plans to renovate the Hermitage, he made notes to order all furnishings from Hurwitz Mintz. Later, he went to Hurwitz Mintz himself to personally select furniture from their fine stock for choice pieces. BF

Directions 55

On the same side of the street at 201 Royal Street corner is Mr. B's Bistro, the former location of Solari's Grocery, or Solan's Grocery.

Solan's Grocery

Solari's Grocery, Importers of Wines, Liquors, Oils, Fruits and Fancy Groceries, was established by brothers Angelo M. and Joseph B. Solari in 1863. It's not clear if the family attempted to Americanized its name by changing it to Sloan or if the name alteration was a result of printing equipment ink blending the "r i" creating an "n". What is known is the brothers began their business by selling to cotton and sugar plantations. Solari's was the epitome of a food emporium, carrying a variety of teas and coffees, and a staggering array of delicacies and spices from around the world.

Solari's kept most products out of the consumers' reach, in display cases. Each shopper had a courteous assistant who handled and packed the product. Having your groceries delivered from Solari's was a sign of wealth. For years, groceries were delivered by a shiny, black horse-drawn coach. Solari's Grocery also had a large mail-order patronage.

The store was extremely successful and once occupied four floors of the building that once stood on this corner. In 1860, a fire completely destroyed the store, but the store was rebuilt. The rebuilt building was demolished in the 1960s and rebuilt again. Since 1979, Mr. B's Bistro has made this corner home.

> A deliveryman from Solan's Grocery was scared out of his wits when he saw wild-eyed Deirdre Mayfair with Lasher by the pool at 1239 First Street. WH

Tidbit – Restaurants

> Arthur Langtry met Irwin Dandrich, the socialite spy for hire, for dinner at a fashionable French Quarter restaurant. WH

> Beatrice Mayfair took Antha and Deirdre, who was a baby, to lunch at a fashionable French Quarter restaurant. WH

> Stella took Antha to breakfast every morning at a different hotel in the French Quarter. WH

> Stella and Lionel Mayfair had had a row in a downtown restaurant and Lionel walked out on Stella. WH

Directions 56

Continue walking up Royal Street and stop when you get to Canal Street. Take a good look at the building across the street at 700-705 Canal Street. The white ornate building on the corner was once a billiard hall on the first floor and the Pickwick Club, a private club, upstairs. Cross the street when it's safe for a closer look.

Pickwick Club

The building was built in 1826. The Merchant's Hotel and a statue of orator Henry Clay were the primary tenants of this corner for many years. The building was remodeled in 1865, but was considered by most to be a simple building with a simple design. Colonel Albert Walter Merriam converted the first floor of the building into an enormous billiard hall and contracted with Henry Howard for a more elaborate exterior design. In 1875, the corner-building exterior became the elaborate Italianate-style structure you see today. In its heyday, the Crescent Billiard Hall was the largest billiard parlor in the world.

The Pickwick Club, a secret society founded in 1857 by a group of prominent young men from the Garden District, took over the second floor of the building in 1950. The club was named after a club in Charles Dickens' first novel, The Posthumous Papers of the Pickwick Club (also known as The Pickwick Papers). For years, a statue of the main character, Mr. Samuel Pickwick, in a black frock coat, gaiters, red vest, and breeches, stood at the entrance to greet guests. Members of the Pickwick Club had a hand in the founding of the Mardi Gras Carnival society, Mystick Krewe of Comus.

> ▶ Julien Mayfair and Judge Daniel McIntyre were members of several exclusive clubs and entertained lavishly during Mardi Gras season. Julien was most likely a member of the Pickwick Club. WH

> ▶ Anne Rice mentions the Mystic Krewe of Comus at least six times in The Witching Hour. WH

Tidbit - Canal Street

Here's a little tidbit about Canal Street. This name was not included in de Pauger's original nomenclature. Its earliest name was Canal des Pecheurs, meaning "the Fisherman's Canal." Canal Street was intended to be a working canal for New Orleans. Like so many city plans, it never materialized. The area became known as the "neutral ground" and the main shopping street for everyone, no matter what race, religious, or status they were. Indians, fishermen, and tradesmen sold their goods and trade in the middle of the nonworking canal before it became an official street. In 1830, its banks were designated la promenade publique (a place for walking, or public walk); a place where the socially elite strolled while fishermen plied their trade in the middle of the "street." The rich, not wanting to mingle with the lower class on the neutral ground, established their own boundaries, and promenades were created on both sides of the canal for the wealthy to stroll. Stores catering to the wealthy soon followed.

- When Lestat switched bodies with Raglan James, none of the clothes in his closet could fit his new body. Lestat, with David Talbot at his side, shopped on Canal Street. BT

- Michael's mother would go out of her way to avoid shopping on Magazine Street. She would pay her fare of seven cents and take the streetcar downtown to shop on Canal Street. WH

- The Mayfair's shopped on Canal Street.

French, Spanish and American Streets

For the next four blocks the streets name may be confusing. Canal Street is one of the widest streets in the United States. It is also the dividing line between the French Quarter, where the French and Spanish lived, and the American Sector, the area the Americans move to after the Louisiana Purchase. The two cultures were not interested in mixing and Canal Street became the dividing line that separated the two cultures.

With a new area, American Sector, came Americanized street names because the Americans did not want to use the French and Spanish names. The French and Spanish felt the same way. The French and Spanish could live with each other but they refused to live with the Americans. As a result, the French Quarter Street names change when you cross Canal Street. They wanted the division of Canal Street to be obvious. The streets name changes you will see on this tour are as follows:

- Royal Street becomes St. Charles Ave
- Bourbon Street becomes Carondelet Street
- Dauphine Street becomes Baronne Street
- Burgundy Street becomes University Place

Kolb's Restaurant

Standing at the corner of St. Charles Avenue and Canal Streets look down St. Charles Avenue and you will see the sign for Kolb's Restaurant, where Dr Cornell Mayfair was to meet Cortland Mayfair for dinner. Kolb's Restaurant is part of our streetcar tour.

Directions 57

Look across the street at the building with the Astor Hotel sign on the roof, currently McDonald's and Radio Shack (709-723 Canal Street) are the primary tenants. This was once the home of Marks Isaacs Department Store.

Marks Isaacs

Marks Isaacs was a German-born merchant, real estate investor, and philanthropist. Isaacs owned several department stores on Canal Street before opening his most famous store. He went from working for his uncle to working in several of the most successful dry good establishments on Canal Street, including Maison-Blanche, before opening the store that bears his name. Marks Isaacs Department Store was located between Royal and Bourbon Streets, in the middle of the old Touro Block, from 1904 until they closed during the 1960s. The store sold clothing and household goods and had an excellent shoe-repair department. Surprisingly, Marks Isaacs was considered to be one of the city's smaller department stores compared to its other rivals on Canal Street. Over the years, the Hotel Astor expanded, acquiring most of the old Touro Block.

The Astor Crowne Plaza Hotel now occupies the building where Marks Isaacs once stood. One of Isaacs' real estate properties and personal residences occupies an entire block uptown. It's currently the Milton Latter Memorial Library, a branch of the New Orleans Public Library system. Isaac's uptown home is part of the streetcar tour.

> Ancient Evelyn used to take the Streetcar downtown to shop at Marks Isaacs. She stopped taking the streetcar after nearly falling one night when she was coming home. She dropped her sacks and the conductor had to come and help her up. LS

Directions 58

Walk down Canal Street towards the main entrance, which is 739 Canal Street, of the Astor Crowned Plaza Hotel. The Astor Hotel entrance and main lobby used to be F. W. Woolworth Company.

F. W. Woolworth Co

When you walk through the entrance doors of the Astor Crowne Plaza Hotel, you are walking inside the old Woolworth store. F.W. Woolworth was found by Frank

Winfield Woolworth and had approximately fifty-seven stores throughout the United States at one time. Woolworth had two stores in New Orleans between 1901-1929, the years Stella was alive. One location was on the ground floor of the eight-story Audubon Building at 1031-1041 Canal Street, which is now part of the Ritz-Carlton Hotel. The second store opened in the 1920s, on the downtown river corner of Bourbon Street, which is now part of the Astor Crowne Plaza Hotel. The store once burned down and was rebuilt. The store was demolished around the same time the old Marks Issacs space was demolished. As the Astor Crowne Plaza Hotel expanded, it acquired the space that was once F.W. Woolworth.

> When Rowan went missing and the legacy house inventoried, the emerald necklace was not found. Despite everything going on, Lauren Mayfair, a lawyer, asked Michael if he knew where the emerald was. Fielding, who was besides himself that Lauren would ask Michael this question, offered to go to Woolworth's and buy a piece of green glass. Lauren, in her characteristic lawyer fashion, let everyone know its whereabouts was a legal issue. LS

Directions 59

Directly across the street from F. W. Woolworth Company at 732 Canal Street was Katz & Besthoff (K & B) Drugstore.

Katz and Besthoff (K&B) Drugstore

This was the location of K&B's first Katz & Besthoff Drugstore. Katz and Besthoff were a well-known drug and convenient store chain that was established in 1905 by Gustave Katz and Sydney J. Besthoff (both registered pharmacists). Originally, they filled prescriptions, sold convenience items, and had a very busy soda/ice cream counter. During the store's 92-year evolution (from 1905 to 1997), they saw several changes from the store's name, from Katz & Besthoff to K&B Drug Store, and continued on to selling their own brand of ice cream, nectar soda, and film processing.

The color "K&B Purple" became part of New Orleans' lexicon, although the K&B Drug Stores are no longer in business. Rite Aid purchased the chain and building leases in 1997, and the famous K&B purple signs disappeared.

> ▶ Cortland Mayfair purchased Christmas tree ornaments and lights to put on the Christmas tree at 1239 First Street for three-year-old Deirdre Mayfair from Katz and Besthoff (K&B) Drug Store. WH

Directions 60

At the corner of Carondelet and Canal Streets is the last, and for locals, the unofficial first, St. Charles Streetcar stops.

St. Charles Streetcar Stop

The first public transit in America began in New York, about 1827. It was called an omnibus, which can be described as a cross between a stagecoach and a mini-streetcar drawn by horses or mules. They traveled along predetermined routes and charged a fare. Around 1832 the omnibus was placed on rails, like trains, and people call it a horse-drawn streetcar and later one word "streetcar". This method of public transportation soon found its way to New Orleans.

Native New Orleanians do not use the term "trolley car". They make their distinction based on the early (1835) definition; a streetcar is always a single car. A trolley car can be a single car or a group of connected cars. The St. Charles Streetcar is the oldest continuously operating streetcar in the world.

- Lestat, wanting his own copy of "Interview with the Vampire" rode the rickety old St. Charles streetcar from the Garden District to the last streetcar stop to buy his book at DeVille Book Store. VL

- Mona and Pierce caught the St Charles Streetcar on the corner of Carondelet and Canal, amid the common crowd. Mona did not think Pierce had ever taken a streetcar in his life. LS

- Michael Curry's mother would take the St Charles Streetcar to Canal Street to avoid shopping on Magazine Street. WH

- Michael Curry and his mother would take the streetcar downtown to see the Saturday matinee movie at the Civic Theater. WH

▸ For fifty years Carlotta Mayfair walked from First and Chestnut Streets to St. Charles Avenue where she caught the St. Charles Streetcar to her job at a downtown law firm on Carondelet Street. WH

▸ Ancient Evelyn and several Mayfair family members used to take the streetcar downtown to shop and do business. LS

▸ The Mayfair's law firm was two blocks off Canal Street on Carondelet Street, by the last streetcar stop. WH

Tidbit - Mary Beth Office

▸ Mary Beth had a secret office downtown. WH

▸ Don't forget our Anne Rice Streetcar tour. You will see many many more places along the streetcar route mentioned in Anne's novels.

Directions 61

Across the street from the streetcar stop, where CVS Pharmacy is today, was Gus Mayer.

Gus Mayer

Located on the corner of Carondelet and Canal Streets is the former New Orleans flagship store of Gus Mayer Department Store. From the corner of the streetcar stop, look up toward the rear of the store roof to your left. You can see the store name on the top of the building toward the rear. Along the top wall of the store you will see more signs for Gus Mayer. Go to the store entrance. Look down and you will see the GM entwined letters.

The store became extremely popular and grew to twenty stores located throughout the United States. Gus Mayer's most famous location was the corner of Canal and Carondelet

Streets, from 1949-1987. These stores specialized in ladies and children's furnishings. CVS adapted the building, which had been constructed during the latter half of 1948.

From the streetcar stop, look up towards the rear of the store to your left; you can see the distinctive Gus Mayer logos, four-leaf clovers, and shield/emblem on the top of the building from the street. Along the top wall you see more signs of Gus Mayer signature artwork. From a safe distance in front of the store look at shield over the front door. Go to the store entrance. Look down and you will see the GM entwined letters on the sidewalk.

- Miss Millie and Miss Belle often went shopping together on Mondays, taking a taxi from First Street to Gus Mayer. WH

- Miss Belle and Miss Millie took Deirdre with them to shop at Gus Mayer. WH

Directions 62

Cross Canal Street and walk down Bourbon Street. Stop at 209 Bourbon Street, Galatoire's Restaurant.

Galatoire's Restaurant

In operation for more than a hundred years and passed down through four generations, this is one of the five best restaurants in the country. The recipes used at Galatoire's came from France along with founder Jean Galatoire.

Galatoire bought an existing restaurant, Victor's, and changed its name to Galatoire's. The restaurant became famous for tasty seafood, as well as tasty meat and chicken dishes. Once Jean's restaurant was established, he sent for his three nephews from southern France to join him in the business. In the early days, Galatoire's did not advertise nor accept reservations. Their patronage grew by word of mouth, and people grew curious about the long lines at the door. It was common for the same waiter to have served a family for generations.

Few things have changed from the early days. The "no reservations" policy has changed slightly. The first floor still maintains the "no reservations" policy. However, Galatoire's does accept reservations for its second floor dining room. Over the decades, celebrities who once joined the queue include Tennessee Williams, Harpo Marx, and Mick Jagger. Galatoire's grandchildren now own and operate the restaurant.

> Aaron Lightner took Richard Llewellyn for a late lunch at Galatoire's. WH

> The Mayfair's took Rowan to lunch here, after she signed legal documents and became the new designee. WH

> Beatrice Mayfair had lunch with Aaron Lightner here and spent three hours talking nonstop. WH

> David Talbot, Aaron Lightner, and a very young Merrick Mayfair dined here. MR

▷ The Mayfair family took Antha to a late lunch at Galatoire's when she became the designee. WH

Directions 63

Continue walking until you get to the corner of Bourbon and Bienville Streets, Desire Oyster Bar, 300 Bourbon Street.

Desire Oyster Bar

Back in 1721, this block of land was twelve lots with houses, stables, gardens, courtyards, and carriageways. Over the years, several businesses have operated on the site, including a winery. In 1890, the American Brewing Company purchased the winery and expanded its holding on the block, creating a business that fronted three streets—Bourbon, Bienville, and Conti. During Prohibition, the American Brewing Company briefly became the American Beverage Company. When Prohibition ended, they went back to being the American Brewing Company. The buildings were demolished in

1964. Several years later, construction began on the Royal Sonesta Hotel, which includes the Desire Oyster Bar. Desire, set against the historic landscape of the French Quarter, is a relative newcomer to the restaurant scene, opening in 1969. The name was taken from the play A Streetcar Named Desire. The Desire Streetcar line was established in 1920 and discontinued in 1948.

> Just before taking a romantic walk through the French Quarter, Michael Curry and Rowan Mayfair had dinner—a searing hot gumbo full of shrimp and andouille sausage, and ice-cold beer at the Desire Oyster Bar. WH

> Aaron Lightner, who was in New Orleans for Nancy Mayfair's funeral, took Rita Mae Lonigan to the Desire Oyster Bar. WH

Directions 64

Return to Canal Street via Bourbon Street. Turn right and walk to 819 Canal Street, D. H. Holmes.

D. H. Holmes

In 1849, its namesake, Daniel Henry Holmes, founded D. H. Holmes Department Store. The store went on to become one of the oldest stores in New Orleans, maintaining its business on Canal Street for approximately 140 years. Holmes eventually expanded to a nationwide chain of stores. This was not bad for a company that started out as a dry goods emporium on Canal Street. The store had very popular lunch counters that served the best meals in town. D. H. Holmes pioneered home delivery service. No matter how small the item, shoppers never had to carry their purchases home. They also had the "must-see" Christmas display on Canal Street. For Mardi Gras, they erected the initials of various parade organizations in lights above the store entrance.

Under the D. H. Holmes clock is a statue of Ignatius Reilly (a character of the Pulitzer Prize–winning A Confederacy of Dunces) waiting for his mother, dressed in a hunting cap, flannel shirt, baggy pants, and scarf.

The D. H. Holmes building became the Chateau Sonesta Hotel in 1989. It was renamed the Chateau Bourbon in 2008, and in 2012 it was renamed Hyatt French Quarter.

- Rita Mae Lonigan bought Deirdre a white silk negligee from D. H. Holmes. WH

- Miss Millie and Miss Belle would often have lunch at D. H. Holmes after a day of shopping. On several occasions Beatrice Mayfair and Ancient Evelyn joined them. WH

- Michael's father bought him a chess set from D. H. Holmes. WH

- Roger took Dora shopping at D. H. Holmes. MD

Directions 65

Return to Bourbon and Canal Streets and cross to the other side of Canal Street when it's safe to do so. Turn right and walk until you get to 828 Canal Street, Godchaux's.

Godchaux's

This store was the brainchild of Leon Godchaux, a French immigrant. Godchaux got his start selling notions before opening his first dry goods store. Around 1865 he had stores in several French Quarter locations, including Decatur Street and Canal Street near Chartres. In the beginning, Leon's stores customarily made and sold men's clothing. Godchaux used some of his profits to buy plantations and became a prominent sugar merchant with nearly fourteen plantations. It was Godchaux's grandson who opened the store at 826-828 Canal Street in 1926 and expanded the business to include women's and children's clothing, jewelry, linens, and home accessories. Business was so good, the Godchaux family expanded their business until the store not only occupied prime retail space on Canal Street, but also occupied a portion of Baronne Street. The new store catered to the middle and upper classes. The store eventually moved to the suburbs and had to change their business structure in order to cater to their new market. They did not survive. The company filed for bankruptcy in 1986, and all the stores were closed. The decorative ironwork remains part of the exterior architecture of the original location.

Miss Millie and Miss Belle shopped at Godchaux's for themselves and family members. Their favorite shopping days were Mondays. WH

Directions 66

Continue walking down Canal Street until you get to the corner of Baronne and Canal Streets. Cross the street back to the French Quarter when it is safe to do so. The huge white building on the corner was once Maison Blanche, 921 Canal Street.

Maison Blanche

Maison Blanche was the first department store to open on Canal Street in 1897. Before Maison Blanche built their store here, the Christ Church stood on this spot, and the area was mostly residential with sprawling mansions. Maison Blanche translates as "white house" in French, and it was the biggest house in the area. The first store was five stories tall, which was the height of most buildings on Canal Street. The store had a massive dome that made it stand out from the other mansions and stores on Canal Street. As years passed, more and more stores expanded, and the mansions were replaced with retail stores. Between 1906 and 1908 the original store was torn down and a new expanded store was built in its place. The new store was considered a skyscraper in its day. The new Maison Blanche building consisted of the main store on the first five floors, with office and medical spaces above the fifth floor. Maison Blanche closed its Canal Street doors in 1982, but reopened for a brief time in 1984. Maison Blanche is now part of the New Orleans Ritz-Carlton Hotel.

- Ancient Evelyn used to take the streetcar downtown to shop at Maison Blanche; the same store other Mayfair relations shopped. LS

- Mona's mother, Alicia, sixteen at the time, left Mona, who was three at the time, in Maison Blanche. Mona did not care. She had fun riding the escalators up and down and doing other things in the store which kept her amused. LS

Directions 67

Continue down Canal Street until you get to 931 Canal Street. This building was once the Kress 5 & 10 Store.

S.H. Kress & Company

Samuel Henry Kress opened his first store in 1887. He went on to open a chain of stores, calling them S.H. Kress & Company. This building, which has French details with a glazed architectural white terra cotta face, was design by Emile Weil, a prominent New Orleans architect. The unique designed can be credited to Kress who insisted his store designs be "works of public art" that would contribute to the cityscape. Kress collected Italian Renaissance and European artwork and founded the Kress Art Collection. Many pieces from his collection are on display in the New Orleans Museum of Art.

Directions 68

Step back and take a look at the two iconic buildings, Maison Blanche and Kress 5 & 10 Store. The buildings were re-purposed to create the massive Ritz-Carlton Hotel.

The Ritz-Carlton

Described as quite luxurious, and in the thick of things, the Ritz-Carlton is a massive hotel. It had its grand opening on October 6, 2000, in the old Maison Blanche Department Store building. The hotel has expanded over the years, repurposing several historic buildings, Kress and Maison Blanche, becoming one of the largest hotels in New Orleans. The hotel takes up three-fourths of the city block, if not more, on Canal Street. In addition to being a combination of several stores with addresses from 901 to 921 Canal Street, it is also a combination of three hotels: Ritz-Carlton, Maison-Orleans, and Iberville Suites.

When Merrick Mayfair made plans to hold an exorcism to get rid of Goblin, the Ritz-Carlton is one of the hotels she suggested the Blackwood farm family stay at until the ritual was completed. BF

Lestat and Quinn Blackwood sensed two rogue vampires, male and female, were staying in a room on the fifteenth floor. The female was Mona's first kill. Quinn killed the male. Once the rogue vampires were dead, Lestat destroyed their bodies with his firepower gift. BC

Directions 69

Continue down Canal Street until you get to the corner of Canal and Rampart Streets. Stop here and look towards the opposite corner of Canal Street, uptown-down lake corner, and you will see what is left of the Loew's State Palace Theatre, 1108 Canal Street.

Tidbit - Loew's State Palace Theatre

Loew's State Palace Theatre, was once one of New Orleans performing art houses with a seating capacity of 3,335 . Two hurricanes and neglect has taken a toll on the building. State Theatre flooded when Hurricane Katrina caused a major levee failure and disaster in 2005. Hurricane Isaac did not help the neglected theatre. The building is in need of major repairs and/or renovations.

> Anne Rice Fan Club 1999 Vampire Ball was there.

Directions 70

Continue down Canal Street until you get to the corner of Canal and Basin Streets.

Union Station

The New Orleans Terminal Company was better known as the Southern Railway Station. Most people called it Union Station or the train station. It once was located between at Canal and Basin Streets. Before this area was a railway station it was the turning basin for the Carondelet Canal. The basin was filled around 1938 and homes and businesses were built on the land surrounding the basin. Southern Railway took advantage of this improvement and built a railroad route over the established basin path and operated on this site from the 1920s to 1954, when the train station was demolished. The Old Union Station and central passenger terminal were consolidated into one location not too far from here.

- When Michael's Aunt Vivian came to New Orleans to visit his mother in 1952, they met her at the Old Union Station. WH

- Louis returned to New Orleans with Armand via the train station. VL

- Members of Michael Curry's family dug the canals and worked on the railroads. WH

- Langtry Arthur left New Orleans immediately after Stella's death via Southern Railway Station. WH

- Aaron Lightner was nearly run down by a taxi outside Union Station when he returned from Texas where he visited Deirdre. WH

- Aaron Lightner departed New Orleans via Union Station after his meeting with Cortland Mayfair. WH

Directions 71

Turn right on Basin Street and walk one block to Iberville and Basin Streets. This area was once Storyville, the Prostitution District. For safety reasons, we ask you to look across the street, but not cross the street at this time.

Storyville

Storyville was established in 1897 by Sidney Story. Knowing that prostitution was rife in New Orleans, Story decided that the city government should allocate a legalized red light district. Containing prostitution to this one area meant that people knew where to go if they wanted a prostitute, and those who didn't simply kept away. Storyville was just a couple of blocks inland from the French Quarter, bordered by Customhouse (Iberville), Basin, St. Louis, and Robertson Streets. Customers could choose from a variety of brothels, using one of several guides called blue books. Two of the most infamous brothels were Lulu White's Mahogany Hall (immortalized in "Mahogany Hall Stomp" by Louis Armstrong) and Josie Arlington's Hall. Interesting enough, most of these establishments were located next to the train station.

Storyville is also responsible for many of the great jazz musicians such as King Oliver, Jelly Roll Morton, Louis Armstrong, Tony Jackson, and Jimmie Noone, who all got their start inside Storyville brothels. The U.S. Navy closed Storyville in 1917 during World War I, and most of the infamous brothels were razed. The razed brothels were replaced by the Iberville public housing project. The Storyville historical marker (256) was once located on the "neutral ground" (median) of Basin Street. It too is gone.

▸ Julien took Mary Beth (dressed like a man), to Lulu White's and Josie Arlington's Hall in Storyville. WH

▸ Mary Beth met her husband, Daniel McIntyre, at Countess Willie V. Piazza House in Storyville. WH

> Manfred Blackwood met Rebecca, his mistress, in Storyville. BF

> Julien took Richard Llewellyn to Lulu White's Mahogany Hall and introduced him to the better houses operating in Storyville. WH

Tidbit - Razzy Dazzy Jazzy

Julien and Mary Beth Mayfair would roam Storyville to catch performances by a group of young street urchins (children who spent most of their time in the streets) called the "Razzy Dazzy Spasm Band". These kids performed with homemade instruments in the streets of Storyville from about 1895 to the early 1900s. When a promoter put together another band and advertised them as the "Razzy Dazzy Spasm Band", the original band members showed up at their Haymarket Dance Hall performance and pelted the stage with rocks. The promoter's advertisement was changed to the Razzy Dazzy Jazzy Band. This was the first time the word jazz was used in printed advertisement in connection with Jazz music.

Directions 72

Continue down Basin Street and look across the street until you see the St. Louis Cemetery No. 1. Cross the street when it is safe to do so.

St. Louis Cemetery 1

In 1789, St. Louis Cemetery became the new cemetery of New Orleans, opening a year after the Great Fire. Two more St. Louis Cemeteries opened in the later years. The above-ground vaults constructed to hold the dead became characteristic of New Orleans. Some say they were designed this way because of the ground water levels; others say it was simply because this was how the Spanish (who ruled the city at this time) buried their dead, so they continued their tradition. It's also been noted that the vaults in St. Louis Cemetery #1 are very similar to those found in Pere Lachaise Cemetery in Paris. This could have been the result of the French residents' influence in New Orleans.

This cemetery is a fraction of the size of the original cemetery, which stretched to Our Lady of Guadalupe Church on

Rampart Street. What is interesting about the burials that occurred here is that people from all walks of life, rich and poor, all cultures, and all colors are buried in St. Louis Cemetery #1. The only form of segregation was by religion, because St. Louis Cemetery #1 is a Roman Catholic cemetery. Different parts of the cemetery were designated for religions other than Roman Catholic.

- Louis, his mother, brother Paul, and other family members are buried here. IV

- Louis once put Armand's coffin next to his crypt, but later removed and destroyed Armand's coffin. IV

- Louis took Lestat on a pilgrimage to his grave here. QD

- Honey in the Sunshine and Cold Sandra were buried here. MR

- Little Ida was buried with her family here. BF

- Two rouge vampires, whom Lestat destroyed with his fire gift, had planned to sleep in the old tombs of St. Louis Cemetery. MK

Tidbit - Visitor Center

As you leave the cemetery look to your left and you will see the New Orleans Visitor's Center. The building looks like it was once a passenger station, but it was never a passenger station. It was the office building for the train station and where people picked up packages sent by train.

This is a great place to take a break. If you need to use the bathroom or get water, you can do so here. They also have many pamphlets for other things you can do in New Orleans.

Directions 73

If you take a break at the visitor's center, you need to walk back to St. Louis Cemetery entrance gate. If you did not take a break, continue on with the tour.

When it is safe to cross the street do so and go to Our Lady of Guadalupe Church, 411 North Rampart.

Our Lady of Guadalupe Church

Our Lady of Guadalupe Church, also known as The Mortuary Chapel of St. Anthony of Padua, is the oldest church in New Orleans. The church dates back to 1826. When yellow fever raged through New Orleans, funerals were banned from St. Louis Church, another historic New Orleans Catholic church. Believing that even in death, yellow fever could be spread, the Our Lady of Guadalupe Church was built to hold its victims. While the St. Louis Cathedral is considered by many to be the oldest Catholic Church in New Orleans, Our Lady of Guadalupe takes the title because the original structure that was St. Louis Church had been torn down and rebuilt.

In 1903, the Dominicans came to New Orleans parish. Father Lorene led the Dominicans as they expanded the Catholic faith and churches throughout the area. Although Father Lorente's work reinvigorated Our Lady of Guadalupe his death caused the church to be abandoned. A fire in 1944 caused damage to the church and rectory. In 1950, the roof timbers collapsed during a heavy rain. The church was rebuilt and stands strong today.

> ▸ The undertakers believed that there should be a Roman Catholic Mass at Our Lady of Guadalupe Church for Great Nananne. Merrick informed them that they didn't need to have a Mass for Great Nananne. MR

Directions 74

When you leave Our Lady of Guadalupe, cross Rampart Street when it is safe to the French Quarter Section. If you are facing the French Quarter, turn left when you get to the corner. If you are facing the church, turn right and walk down the Rampart Street, away from Canal Street to Toulouse Street and stop.

Charity Hospital

Charity Hospital was between Toulouse and St. Peter Streets. In 1726 the Ursuline nuns arrived in New Orleans and assumed responsibility for much of the decent medical care for non-military colonists, orphans, poor, slaves, and Indians from the Royal (military) Hospital. The nuns' hospital, first established in the French Quarter, was the first Charity Hospital. For several years, the nuns and Royal Hospital shared the same facilities. The nuns were not happy with this arrangement and lobbied for their own facility. Between 1734 and 1779, Charity and Royal Military Hospitals were destroyed by either fire or hurricanes.

In 1785, another Charity Hospital was built and named Hospital of Saint Charles (the San Carlos Hospital) but was also known as Almonaster Hospital (named after its benefactor). Unofficially, it was known as the third Charity Hospital, because it was built on the same spot as the previous (second) Charity Hospital between Toulouse and St. Peter Streets on N. Rampart Street. It also served as the Spanish Military Hospital or the old King's Hospital. However, there were very few sick soldiers and government officials in New Orleans at the time. Only the "poor in real distress" were admitted, unless a daily fee was paid. The hospital was destroyed by fire in 1809.

The third Charity Hospital is mostly likely the hospital where Lestat left Claudia. When Lestat and Louis went walking, Louis said that Lestat led him far from the main part of the old town, and they were near the ramparts. IV

Directions 75

Look across the street from where Charity Hospital used to be. That's the Tremé neighborhood.

The Ramparts - Back of Town - Tremé

The Ramparts were the original defensive fortifications of the French colonial city wall, built to protect the city against invasion, and were situated on the north side of the street. The ramparts guarded the city from the rear with two forts. Fort St. Jean stood at the intersection of N. Rampart and Barracks Streets on one side and Fort Bourgogne stood at the intersection of N. Rampart and Iberville Streets on the other side. At Old Bayou Road (now Governor Nicholls Street) there was also protection for the city and a passage that led out of the city through a gate.

The forts were decommissioned around 1823. For many years, the area opposite the city's protected walls (lakeside of Rampart Street) was referred to as the Ramparts or "back of town". Today, the area is known as Tremé, one of the oldest neighborhoods in the city, and early in the city's history was the main neighborhood of free people of color. Louis Armstrong Park, the Municipal Auditorium and the area surrounding these iconic sites are all part of the Tremé neighborhood.

North Rampart Street was known as Love Street up until 11/20/1852. It's said that young men maintained homes for their quadroon mistresses between Bayou Road and Dumaine Street off of Love Street.

> When Lestat made Louis a vampire, he did not have an extra coffin. The one coffin Lestat did have was, according to Louis, in a miserable room near the Ramparts, and they had to share it. IV

- Lestat led Louis to the Ramparts and the hospital where they found Claudia still alive, after Louis fed off her. IV

- The mother and daughter servants who were killed by Claudia and left in the courtyard oven lived in the Ramparts with their family. IV

Directions 76

Continue walking down Rampart Street until you get to St. Ann Street. Turn left. You will see Armstrong Park and Congo Square, cross the street when it is safe to do so. Continue to the big building you see to your left, Municipal Auditorium.

Municipal Auditorium

The Municipal Auditorium and Concert Hall was the primary entertainment center in New Orleans for many years. Originally known as the Municipal Auditorium and Exhibition Hall, it was built to fill the void of the French Opera House, which had burned to the ground in 1919. The building was commission in 1929, when Arthur J. O'Keefe was mayor, and dedicated May 30, 1930 as a memorial to the dead heroes of the World War I.

The historic Italian Renaissance Revival-style building has foundations and walls of rusticated limestone. It has played host to operas, dance recitals, graduation ceremonies, carnival balls, pageants, sporting events, auto shows, conventions, and concerts (including the Beatles and Elvis Presley), as well as the music festival that grew into the New Orleans Jazz and Heritage Festival, among other festivities.

The building was officially renamed the Morris F.X. Jeff Municipal Auditorium in 1994, after a teacher and coach. The Auditorium was renovated and transformed into a multi-purpose arena and auditorium. At one time, the auditorium was one of the largest buildings in the city.

The auditorium sits on land that was once part of a water basin. When the land was filled in and the railroad built its track over the filled-in basin, homes and shops catering to black people who lived in this area soon followed. When the Auditorium was built, it displayed many Africa-American people, some who had lived in the area for generations.

A special event in Michael Curry's life was a concert at the Municipal Auditorium. Michael had never seen the Municipal Auditorium. His father, who took extra jobs in his time off, was working there one night to make extra money. Michael went along to help his daddy, and finally got a chance to see the Municipal Auditorium. WH

Conclusion

This concludes our tour. Take your time and enjoy Armstrong Park and Congo Park. When you are finished, cross back to French Quarter. St. Ann Street is one block to your right or left, depending on where you exit the auditorium.

Directions 77 To Jackson Square

Walk down St. Ann Street. This is the reverse route Louis and Lestat took after they return from Armand's Night Island to Louis grave. St. Ann Street will take you back to Jackson Square.

Discover
And Expand Your
Psychic Powers
In
6 Weeks

Taffy Sealyham

Do you think you have supernatural gifts? Want to develop your psychic abilities? We recommed you read Discover and Expand Your Psychic Powers In 6 Weeks by Taffy Sealyham. You will learn how to find lost objects and how to mediate, telepathy, psychometry, read auras, ESP and more. Maybe you have the same abilities of Vampires or the Mayfair Witches.

CPSIA information can be obtained
at www.ICGtesting.com
Printed in the USA
FFOW04n1319130516
23960FF

9 781938 734038